Copyright 2

MW00818259

ISBN-13: 978-0988332843

TABLE OF CONTENTS

SECTION I

INTRODUCTION TO MIND MAPS

From the time we start kindergarten to the time we graduate college, our schools, teachers, and educational system thrust overwhelming amounts of information at us. They tell us to read this, learn that, write this, and practice that. They shovel information, and we're expected to cope as best as we can. The further we go, the bigger the shovel.

Although our teachers tell us what to learn, they seldom show us how. They never really give us ways to retain, classify, organize, and remember information. Instead, they feed us everything from when the Civil War started to the atomic weight of oxygen. Those who absorb the information are labeled smart. Those that don't are left feeling like they lack the ability to do well in school, and worse, in life. Unless we are very clever or lucky enough to develop study strategies on our own, we never discover the proper ways to learn and remember what we are taught.

To make matters worse, we now live in the information age. We have never been surrounded by as much information as we are today. In fact, Google's executive chairman Eric Schmidt stated that every two days we produce the same amount of information as humans have produced from the dawn of writing to 2003. It is truly staggering how anyone can get a handle, let alone manage all this.

With this constant wave of new knowledge, by the time we master a skill, either more education is required to keep up or the skill becomes obsolete. This is especially prevalent in the IT world, where new programming languages and technologies come into the forefront to replace the old. Even if we wanted to stop learning, we can't for the risk of falling behind in our lives. We are truly in an age where if we are not moving forward, we are moving backward.

Fortunately, an innovative technique for learning and memory exists. It is a powerful method that mimics how the human brain naturally processes, organizes, and stores data. The technique is called *mind mapping* and it is what you'll learn in this book.

CHAPTER 1 - WHAT IS A MIND MAP

• A mind map is a note-taking tool that organizes words, thoughts, ideas, tasks, activities, and more in the form of a diagram. The diagram starts with a key or main idea in the center with subtopics radially around the main idea. The subtopics group and cluster similar ideas and they branch out to lower and lower-level topics, guiding you to wherever your thought processes lead you.

Below is an example of what it looks like:

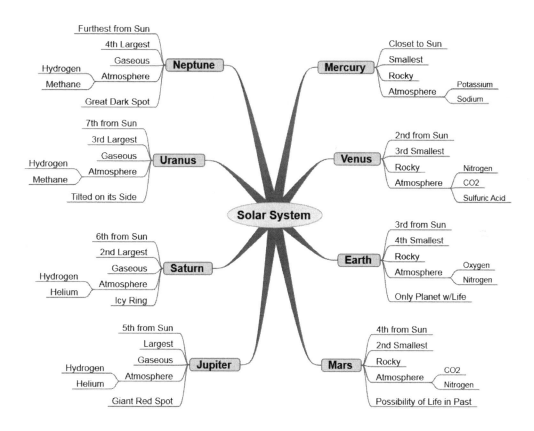

This mind map discusses the planets of the solar system. As you can see, we have the main topic in the middle. Since it is about the solar system, we wrote that as the main topic. Our solar system has 8 planets, so we drew 8 lines branching out from the center. These represent the subtopics. Within each subtopic, we listed specific details about each planet in clusters around that planet. These are the lower-level topics.

This is the fundamental nature of mind maps. You start with a thought, idea, or problem in the middle, and then you branch outward. The design is similar to a tree in that one keyword or idea begins the process, and from there other interconnected and related entities stem.

Mind mapping is not a new concept. It has been around for over a millennium, and legendary intellects such as Leonardo da Vinci and Picasso are known to have utilized the method. More recently, Tony Buzan popularized and systematized the technique in the 1960s and 1970s. In fact, *mind map* and *mind maps* are registered trademarks of Buzan's company. He has written many books and produced several shows about the concept. Since Buzan's work, more and more people have become enthusiastic users of the system.

Benefits of Mind Mapping

Mind maps offer many benefits. For starters, they improve learning and memory by working in line with the associative nature of your brain. In addition, they make it quicker to process and easier to organize information. More importantly, the technique enhances creativity and encourages brevity. We will discuss each of these benefits in detail below.

Associations

Every new thought or idea your brain has or learns needs to connect to other thoughts and ideas. When you learn a new piece of information, that fact doesn't aimlessly float around in your head. Instead, it attaches itself to something else. This is the way your brain works, it connects thoughts, ideas, and experiences to other thoughts, ideas, and experiences. Each thought or idea in your head has hundreds to thousands of links in your mind.

For instance, have you ever seen or heard something while going about your daily life that then prompted a whole set of other memories? The memory is so vivid that you can feel the experience all over again. Perhaps you open the windows early in the morning and smell fresh-cut grass combined with newly-blooming lilacs. Suddenly you are taken back to the past when you were ten years old. Your brother was cutting the lawn while your mother arranged hand-picked lilacs in a vase, and you sneezed at the strong scent. You can feel the moment, and the memory surges back as if it just happened.

This is your brain making a very real association. It is taking the current experience brought on by the smell of newly-blooming lilacs and connecting it to some point when you encountered a similar smell. If your brain were not associative, it would not bring up past experiences this way. In fact, the next time you encounter the smell of lilacs, that experience will more than likely be associated to the current one as well as to the one from your childhood.

As stated, your brain makes such associations with every thought, idea, and experience. When you learned about the Revolutionary War in history class, your mind connected it to guns, fighting, battles, and explosions because that is what movies and books have taught us about war. When you learned about numbers in school, your teacher connected them to quantities of physical objects like the number of crayons in a box. When you were taught the alphabet, she associated each letter with items whose name began with that letter—*a* for apple, *b* for bear. Your teacher did that because in order to understand and retain new bits of data, your brain needs to connect it to something else.

In our solar system example, you can see a mind map follows a similar structure. You start off with a topic or idea in the center, and then you associate other ideas around it. From there, you join even more thoughts and ideas around the subordinate ideas. Each piece of information is always connected to another piece. This is the way mind maps are structured. They bring together information in an associative way, similar to your brain.

Incorporates Sense of Sight

Another benefit of mind maps is that they incorporate your sense of sight. If you look at the above mind map again, more or less it is an image that is processed by the same mechanisms that process sight. And the parts of the brain that processes sight are much quicker and more powerful than the parts that process other types of information. Not only are images quicker to process, but they are easier to remember as well. In 1970, Ralph Haber published research that asserted that people have a recognition accuracy of images between 85 and 95 percent. This is true even if you are not a *visual* person.

To demonstrate, suppose that you work at a gifts and accessory store. A customer walks in asking if you carry a particular keychain, which she describes as follows. She says the keychain has a metal ring where all the keys go. Attached to the metal ring is a flower. The flower is made of leather and has eight petals. The top part of the flower is purplish pink and the bottom is a light pink. The center of the flower is yellowish orange with a metal button in the middle. Also, there is a threaded seam around the edge of each petal.

Although the above description is a detailed, it doesn't give you much to work with. With this narrative, one can conjure up many different types of flowers. You may find the correct keychain or you may not.

What if, however, this person shows you a picture of the keychain? Instead of describing it in words, she says, here is how it looks:

From the above picture, in an instant you know what the keychain looks like and for what you have to search. There is no need for the customer to write a lengthy description. Nor is there a need for you to process that description in an attempt to understand it. The connection is immediate.

Not to mention, there is little room for misinterpretation. Although our description above accurately describes the keychain, it probably wasn't the image that initially came up in your mind. There was likely some disconnect between the customer's words and your interpretation of those words. With images, there is less likelihood of that happening.

Even more, you are likely to remember this image longer and in more detail than the words used to describe the image. Two weeks or even a month down the road, there is a good chance you will still have a clear impression of the picture in your mind. As far as her words, there is a good chance you have already forgotten them.

It's for this reason mind maps are such an amazing tool. Because you are employing a part of the mind that is faster, more powerful, and more efficient, their visual nature makes them easier to process and even easier to remember. By incorporating this aspect into your learning, you can understand information better and remember it longer. If you play video games, you can think of this in terms of the way a graphics card increases the computing power of a computer. Using mind maps is like hooking up the processing power of a graphics card to your brain.

Better Organization of Information

Mind maps make it easier to organize information. In traditional forms of organization, we frequently write information line by line or in the form of an outline. With line-by-line note taking, there is no certainty of linking of information. Facts and ideas may be placed without any care for how they are related or connected to one another, even though we've learned that it's essential for both memory and comprehension to associate facts and ideas with other facts and ideas.

Although outlines do a better job of connecting information, they are limited in design and functionality. If we were to organize our diagram of the solar system into an outline, it would look as follows:

PLANETS

I. Mercury
  A. Position—1st
  B. Type—Rocky
  C. Size—Smallest
  D. Atmosphere
    i. Potassium
    ii. Sodium

II. Venus
  A. Position—2nd

B. Type—Rocky
C. Size—3rd Smallest
D. Atmosphere
    i. Nitrogen
    ii. Carbon Dioxide
    iii. Sulfuric Acid

III. Earth
    A. Position—3rd
    B. Type—Rocky
    C. Size—4th Smallest
    D. Atmosphere
        i. Nitrogen
        ii. Oxygen
    E. Only Planet w/ Life

To keep the illustration simple, this outline summarizes only the first three planets—Mercury, Venus, and Earth. From the outline, you can see that it is well organized. The indents and numbering tell you how ideas are grouped. The first indent lists the planets. The second indent lists features of the planet. From there, each additional indent lists the details of each feature.

Although there is organization in this outline, it is strictly hierarchical. Adding in a new idea requires a whole new numbering scheme. Anyone who has worked on a paper can tell you how troublesome it can be to rearrange information inside an outline, especially in the early stages when you're brainstorming. If you get a sudden surge of creativity, it will be difficult to insert those inspired thoughts. Outlines have their place, but they are not the best option when you need to make on-the-fly alterations.

In contrast, mind maps are both hierarchical and they make it easy to add new information. They are hierarchical in that branches stem from a topic to lower- level ideas to which they are related. You can follow the line to Neptune and find two other ideas attached to it:

Gaseous and *Great Dark Spot*. You can also take an arbitrary fact like *Sulfuric Acid* and follow the line back to the center and find the planet to which it relates—Venus. With this format, the structure of each idea as it relates to others is easily communicated. No matter how complex branches get, you can always follow the hierarchy back to the center by following the line.

Mind mapping makes it easy to add information because we add additional ideas simply by inserting additional branches. If we want to include information about the asteroid belt that lies between Mars and Jupiter, we can create a branch between them. This is in direct contrast to an outline or other methods in which information quickly becomes squashed and difficult to read when new material is added after the fact. Mind map's versatile structure allows the brain to continuously see new associations and to think outside the box, making it easier to link ideas at a later stage.

Also notice the use of color, shapes, and font size. In an outline, these sorts of things aren't used. You might be able to bold a particular item, such as a thesis statement, but the use of color is frowned upon, much less using shapes. Therefore you are limited to indentations and variety in numbering when trying to organize your facts. Mind maps give you more flexibility. As you will learn in the next chapter, color, shape, and branch size go a long way to help you organize content.

Stimulates Creativity

An important benefit of using a mind map is that it stimulates creativity. Part of the creative process is to let ideas flow and swirl without judgment. That means allowing yourself to record ideas without first deciding whether or not they fit. In problem solving, this is particularly important not only in generating solutions, but elaborating on those solutions. With mind maps, since you are not forced to look at thoughts and ideas in a linear fashion, your mind is free to ramble about, and as a result, can generate more substantive solutions.

Another part of the creative process is being able to bounce around from one idea to the next, adding thoughts or categories as they come up in your mind. Interestingly, ideas in our minds rarely arise in the order we want them. For instance, if you are developing a set of instructions, while working on step 2, you might get a great idea for step 8. The problem is you are not on step 8 yet. You are not even on step 3. A mind map doesn't require that you wait until you get to the 8th step to work out its details. As thoughts surface, you simply create a branch or appropriate level subtopic for that thought. This way, your mind is free to wander back and forth as ideas come up.

Each one of us has a wealth of marvelous ideas rumbling around in our heads, and mind maps empower us to put them into action. The linked relationships we chart can grow to be motivating devices that encourage us to visit and revisit our ideas. We can walk away from our mind maps and come back to them again and again to discover what may be our best hidden inspirations mapped out right before our eyes.

Thrives on Brevity

The main benefit of mind maps is that they are more concise in summarizing and ordering information. One of the ways mind maps accomplish this with the use of keywords. Keywords are words or sets of words that summarize text of longer length into short phrases. Notice that in our solar system mind map, we use short terms with each branch or sub-branch. Instead of saying *Earth has an atmosphere composed of two types of gases, one is Nitrogen and the other Oxygen*, we simply branch out with the keywords *Nitrogen* and *Oxygen*.

The majority of our thinking and notes can be condensed this way. That is, although most of what we read and hear is necessary to understand a subject, it is not necessary when trying to summarize or recall it. To better explain what we mean, let's use this subsection on the *Benefits of Mind Maps* as an example. As you may have noticed, this section employs several pages of lengthy text with some illustrations to help you comprehend why mind maps are so beneficial. We wrote out all these sentences and paragraphs to provide thorough explanations using a variety of analogies and examples to help you and other readers really grasp the core concepts of association, sense of sight, etc.

Once you grasp these core concepts, however, you don't need the entire text to remember what was said. You can recap the segment by saying *mind maps are beneficial because they use associations, incorporate sense of sight, improve organization, enhances creativity, and are more concise.* Once you understand a concept, to remember it, there is no need to recall all of the words and sentences that were used to convey the information. You can simply recall the major points, or *keywords*, from the discussion.

With mind maps, you focus on these keywords and keyword phrases when developing your topics and subtopics. As a result, the information is more succinct. The central idea, and thus the subject of the mind map, becomes clear and is immediately noticeable. Since most of the fluff is omitted, less information needs to be processed and remembered as the remainder of the data is stripped down to the essential elements relating to the subject.

Keywords are not the only aspect of mind mapping that make them brief. The other aspect is that they do not require the use of words to describe relationships or lack thereof. These relationships are established with lines or branches connecting them. For example, in our mind map of the solar system, there is no need to write out *Saturn has an icy ring surrounding the planet.* Since the term *icy ring* stems from Saturn, it is enough to establish the relationship. Also, since this term branches only from Saturn, we know not to confuse it with Jupiter or Uranus. Items for Jupiter and Uranus are in different branches. This applies to the remaining features of the other planets in the diagram.

In standard note-taking, on the other hand, we establish order and relationships by writing down and putting grammar around topics. Mind maps allow us to avoid this extra step. In mind maps, like information stays to together and unlike information stays apart without the use of words to make the connection or distinction. Since much of the irrelevant language that would have been used in traditional note taking to convey the same amount of information is absent, only the salient points represented in graphic form remain.

These are the major advantages of using mind maps. Now that you understand them, let's learn how to apply this technique to improve memory, concentration, communication, organization, creativity, and time management.

CHAPTER 2 - CREATING AND ENHANCING YOUR MIND MAP

Mind maps are fairly easy to put together. You probably have a good idea of how to assemble one based on the overview and discussion of benefits in the previous chapter. Nonetheless, we will go more into depth here. We will discuss not only how to create mind maps, but also how to enhance them with different attributes like colors, branches, and images.

Creating a Mind Map

When creating a mind map, think of the information you want to note in terms of main topic, subtopic, and lower-level topics. These are the principal building blocks. Most information can be broken down and organized into this hierarchy.

1. **Main Topic**—The main topic is the subject you want to map. If you are taking notes of a book or article, the main topic will be its focus or title. If you are performing research, the main topic will be the matter you are researching. If problem solving is what you are looking to do, the main topic will be the problem for which you seek a solution. Place this in the center of the map.

2. **Subtopic**—Subtopics are like subheadings of a chapter in a book. They are the noteworthy components or characteristics of the main thought. For note taking, that might be the important points, or as stated, the subheadings and headers. In research, that may include the relevant facts. In problem solving, each solution or component of a solution might be represented by a subtopic. Draw these radially around the main topic, connecting each one to the center with a line or branch.

3. Lower-Level Topics—The lower-level topics detail or describe the features and traits of the subtopic. Generate these lower-level ideas and branches as you see fit. Remember, you are constructing a hierarchy of ideas instead of random links, so each lower-level thought should relate or belong to a thought higher in the branch. Link them with a line to their corresponding subtopic.

As you go through the above steps, do not over think each thought pattern as if you were creating an outline. You have much more freedom with a mind map. Instead, make associations and then connect them to other ideas. Always keep in mind the relationship of the outside items to the center items. The more important the thought, the closer it should be to the center.

When assembling the map, you can insert information one level at a time or one subtopic at a time. Using the solar system as an example, one level at a time means you first draw out all the branches for the planets before moving to the next level to talk about their features. Alternatively, one subtopic at a time means you focus on one planet, detailing its features and noteworthy facts into lower and lower branches before moving to the next planet.

If you already know what all your subtopics will be—Mercury to Neptune in our example—then it helps to write them out first. This frees your mind to concentrate on the details, allowing you to go from one branch to the next filling in the appropriate facts in the appropriate place. If you are using stream of conscious to assemble the map, though, you will want to go where your thoughts lead you. If your mind is exploding with notes about a particular subtopic, then run with that branch and pile up as many lower-level thoughts as necessary before moving to the next. Don't feel compelled to work within one level or subtopic before moving to the next. Do what feels right in the moment.

As it relates to the direction you place the branches, it helps to draw them clockwise. In our example, we started with Mercury and spiraled rightward as we listed Venus, Earth, Mars, etc. Because of the habits ingrained in us by reading clocks, this is the natural way our mind likes to read circular type information. Now, this may be more difficult to achieve the deeper you go into lower-level branches, but do the best you can.

Finally, focus on keywords or keyword phrases. As you learned in the last chapter, the efficient use of mind maps requires using keywords and associating them with other keywords to summarize information. A good keyword is one that encapsulates or hones in on a concept the best. When you first start mind mapping, the temptation to use complete phrases will be enormous, but you should always look for opportunities to shorten phrases to a single or at most a few words.

Although shortening phrases tends to be easier for main and subtopics, it proves more difficult for lower-level concepts. That's because lower-level ideas detail and describe their higher counterparts. By nature, that requires a longer narrative, which can't always be shortened into a small phrase. Therefore, as you go farther into lower-level branches, you will find it more challenging to condense ideas into keywords. With lower-level branches, it is o.k. to stray from keywords. For main ideas and subtopics, however, you should still focus on abbreviating them as much as possible.

Enhancing Your Map

The mind map of the solar system we presented in the previous chapter is fairly basic in design. We presented it this way to make the essential components of main, sub, and lower-level topics more apparent. However, the beauty of mind maps is that you can get really creative with its structure and layout. You can vary the thickness of branches, add color, and more importantly, you can incorporate images. To illustrate, below is a variation of the solar system map with these attributes:

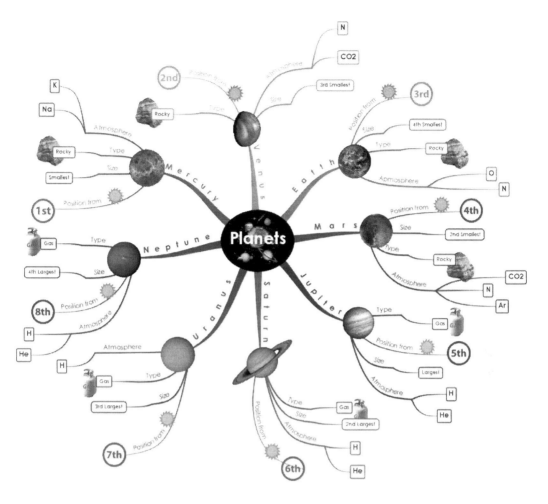

As you can see, this map is much more visual. It is does a better job of grabbing your attention, and to some extent, is more aesthetically pleasing. Let's look at these elements more closely.

Branch Width

Looking at the branches in this map, you will notice the width of the sub-branches is thinner than that of the main branches to which they are connected. Likewise, the width of the lower-level branches is even thinner than that of the sub-branches. This variation in thickness helps to establish hierarchy. When you see a wide branch, like the one stemming from the center of the map to one of the planets, you automatically know that it is related to the main topic and will likely be important. When you see a thinner branch, like the ones with the label *atmosphere* or *size*, you know they are related to and are providing detail about one of the subtopics. Altering the thickness like this helps establish hierarchical precedence.

Color

If you look at our illustration again, you will also notice each subtopic has a unique color. The branches for Jupiter are blue; Saturn is in a dark green, and Uranus is red. This helps us differentiate information residing in different clusters. That is, when we read something in green, we know the description is about Saturn and not about Jupiter or Uranus. In the same manner, when we read anything in red, we know the discussion relates to Uranus, not to Saturn or Neptune. Like thickness of a branch, color can separate related information from unrelated. In this example, it separates one subtopic from another.

Image

Looking at the map one more time, this version incorporates images. For each one of the planets, we placed an image of that planet, and within the lower-level branches, we incorporated other images like that of a gas tank or rock to signify whether the planet is gaseous or rocky. This adds a more visual component to the map. If you remember, anything visual is easier to process and retain, thus increasing your understanding and memory. If on an exam you are asked which planet has a ring of ice, you will have an easier time answering Saturn because you have seen the image with its rings.

By varying width size, color, and incorporating images, it is easy to tell which part of the solar system you are in and where the center of the map resides. You can also differentiate concepts by using different font sizes, different shapes, or anything else you'd like. As long as you know the keys for your map, there's quite a bit you can do to make it your own. Some people doodle in the corners or use dotted line styles as branches. Mind mapping software, a topic we will discuss later in the book, has a set of options for all these. By using them, you can really personalize your map.

This is the nuts and bolts of mind mapping. You start with a thought or idea in the center and then branch outward like a spider web. You can branch one topic at a time or one level at a time. As you branch out, you do your best to summarize concepts into keywords. And with each branch, you can vary the thickness, apply colors, and employ images of various sorts to create memorable visual distinctions.

Getting Started

Now that you have a better understanding of mind maps—what they are, how they work, and their benefits—let's look at the different ways to apply them in different situations. Before getting started though, it is important to point out that because mind maps are free-thinking creations, there is no right or wrong way to do them. The technique is unique to the person creating them. Although this book provides suggestions on what to do, you should take them as merely suggestions and nothing more. What's more important is that you develop your own style and fit it to your own needs.

Another important point to mention is that the mind map examples in the following sections look a little different from what we presented above. Although these mind maps will be heavy in content, they will be a bit basic in design. The reason for this is because on paperback books, images do not display well, especially images of mind maps. The style we use in the subsequent chapters is the most effective for viewing on physical paper. With this style, we are able to provide more detail in the diagram without compromising clarity. Granted, the images may not always look perfect, but you should have an easier time viewing them.

If you still have trouble viewing the images, don't worry too much. With each mind map, we will provide a thorough description of the details. This will help you stay informed as to the set-up and structure of the content within the image.

Now that the important considerations are out of the way, let's get started. We will begin by showing you how to use mind maps for note taking. This is the most widely used function of mind maps. From there, we will show you how to apply them in other areas such as in research, brainstorming, and writing. In this section, you will see the true flexibility of the technique. Then we will discuss other methods similar to mind maps that can prove to be just as useful. After that we will discuss using mind maps with children and computer-assisted mind mapping. Finally we will present creative applications of the tool others have developed. If you are ready, let's get started.

SECTION II

NOTE TAKING WITH MIND MAPS

Note taking is a critical activity for each and every one, whether you are a student listening to a lecture, a consultant understanding a customer's requirements, or even an entrepreneur working on a business plan for capital funding. No matter who you are, what you do, where you come from, or where you are going, at one point or another, you will have to take notes.

Mind maps were created for this exact purpose. This is the essence of the technique. You'll find that majority of your note taking will come from written materials, such as books and articles, and live presentations, such as lectures and seminars. In this section, you will learn how to apply mind maps in both these areas. You will learn how to build successful notes from material you read and content you hear.

The goal of this section is to do more than simply show you how to apply mind maps for note taking. It is to make you a better learner of written and spoken material. Consequently, in the next two chapters, you will also learn the proper ways to read texts and listen to lectures. Combining effective reading and listening techniques with mind maps will help you become more efficient with your notes while getting more out of them.

CHAPTER 3 - TAKING NOTES OF WRITTEN MATERIAL

Mind maps are great for noting written material because they help you gain a more solid understanding of the information you are reading. That is because with ordinary notes, in a sense you simply regurgitate the information. You take what you see written and then you re-write it in summary form. Although the mere act of writing what you want to understand and remember aids learning, it is slow and tedious. When you have page after page and chapter after chapter to learn, it can become too much for your mind to process and retain.

This is one of the main reasons people lose confidence in their intelligence and ability to learn. When someone is unable to understand or recall what they have just read, they assume that it is because they are incompetent. They conclude that the reason they cannot grasp the text must be because they don't mentally have what it takes. This is rarely the case. More often than not, the reader was not active with the information he or she was reading.

Mind maps allow you to be active. When you take notes with this technique, you don't simply regurgitate the information. Creating useful branches and setting appropriate hierarchy requires analyzing the information you are reading. You have to think about how the information is related, where there are differences, when new thoughts begin, and when they end. In this way, you are active in making sense of what you are reading instead of relying on your mind to make sense of it for you. This helps you better understand, use, and recall the material, ultimately improving your ability to learn.

Furthermore, with conventional note taking, there is a tendency for the mind to lose focus and drift on other thoughts. You have probably experienced this quite often. You are diligently reading and writing your notes, only to realize that you were preoccupied by another thought the entire time. Perhaps you were thinking about a conversation you had with a friend or an interesting event that took place at work, or maybe you were mentally planning your weekend getaway. Next thing you know, you have finished pages of text with little idea of what they are about.

Again, mind mapping is an active process. It is not something you do while daydreaming. So when you take notes, you do so with full attention. Even though distracting thoughts may crop up here and there, they will not sidetrack you.

Mind mapping written content requires a systemized approach. The approach includes the following steps, which we will go into detail below.

1. Preview

2. Read

3. Mind Map

4. Review

1. Preview

The first step in mapping a book or article is to preview. Previewing requires taking a few moments to familiarize yourself with the material you are about to read. This means skimming through the book, looking at the table of contents, major headings, words in bold or italics, quoted texts, illustrations, graphs, summaries, and any other important element that catches your eye. The goal is to acquaint yourself with the broad purpose of the content and how it is organized.

Previewing is an important step as it prepares you for what you are about to read. It introduces you to the topics that will be discussed as well as the important points that will be made. It also provides you with a general understanding of the structure of the material. All of this gives you a valuable starting point for your mind map.

Tony Buzan likens previewing to putting together a jigsaw puzzle. To assemble a jigsaw puzzle properly, you have to first look at the box cover. Then you arrange the end pieces. Only then should you fill in the center. Assembling a puzzle this way saves time and energy because it helps you see the big picture. Without some sort of picture, arranging a jigsaw can prove to be quite difficult. The same applies to reading without previewing. In the absence of a recognized structure, the information you read can be difficult to process. In fact, studies suggest that as much as 90% of your understanding of a topic can be gained from this step.

Previewing is also important because it helps you utilize the power of incremental learning. Your mind does not learn everything at once. It learns in steps. When it takes in new information, it needs first to build a foundation. Only when it has a firm foundation can it learn the next step. Only after it has learned the next step can it go further.

Effective teachers know the importance of incremental learning. They don't throw the most complicated information to their students first. They start with the basics and then work up. It is this principle that makes previewing beneficial. It gives your mind a foundation which prepares you to receive new information more easily.

The method used to preview depends on the type and length of the material you are reading. Articles and reports tend to be straightforward, so they do not require too much effort. Books and technical manuals, on the other hand, tend to be longer and more involved, so they require more time at the preview stage. Below are guidelines for how to preview different types of material.

Articles and Reports

Read the first and last paragraphs, examine words in bold or italics, read any quoted texts, and glance at illustrations if there happen to be any.

Books and Manuals

Read the front and back covers. Look at the table of contents to get a feel for the organization of the book. See whether the book is divided into sections or parts (this can represent the first hierarchy). Look at the chapter headings to get a feel for the topics that will be covered.

Then read samples of the text. If there is a preface, begin with that. Next, read the introduction and conclusion. Afterwards, skim through the book and take note of items in bold, italics, quotes, and any diagrams or tables. While skimming, read the first and last paragraphs of each chapter.

Textbooks

The approach to previewing textbooks is similar to books and manuals. However, if you are going to study a textbook, more than likely it will be for a class. That means you will be assigned to read the text one chapter at a time—or even one subheading at a time. So instead of previewing the entire textbook, focus strictly on the area that you are assigned to read.

With textbooks, start with reviewing the chapter objectives. Then read the summaries at the beginning of the chapter. Most text books have review questions at the end of each chapter or section. Read these and keep them in mind. As always, review any and all items in bold, italics, quotes, as well as all illustrations and graphs.

Stories & Novels

Students always ask whether it is necessary to preview stories or novels let alone to mind map them. The answer is that it depends on your purpose. If you are reading a story or novel for pleasure, then more than likely you want to avoid any sort of preview; otherwise you may uncover too much of the plot, or worse, the ending. This takes away from the joy of reading such material.

If you are reading a story or novel because it is an assignment for class and/or you will be tested on your knowledge and understanding of the details, then it would be beneficial to preview and mind map it. In these instances, you should approach the material as normal. Read the front and back cover. Review the table of contents. Skim through the text. With this type of read, you will not find many items in bold or italics, nor many illustrations or graphs. So when skimming, pay attention instead to the plot, setting, the characters and the roles they play.

The above lists the various ways to go about previewing different types of material. Since the preview is only a preparation step, do not spend too much time at this stage. The objective is to simply sample the material, not to go into detail. Therefore, you should spend no more than 45 seconds to 5 minutes when previewing. Typically, this means 45 seconds to two minutes for shorter texts like articles and reports and 3-5 minutes for longer ones like books and manuals.

As mentioned, previewing is critical to the effectiveness of the mind mapping process. In fact, previewing is critical to any reading process. Whether you buy into mind maps or simply prefer linear note taking, try to always preview the material you read. You will find that you can more easily understand and more quickly process the information once you have previewed it. Often, you can get everything you need from this stage, which can save you a lot of time and effort.

2. Read

The next step in the process is to read. This step is fairly straightforward. You read the text as you normally would. You start at the beginning. Then you work your way to the end.

While reading, though, think about how the information can be organized into a mind map. Consider where the connections lie and how they come together. It helps to read with keywords in mind. Look for how paragraphs and sections of text can be summarized into a single word or thought. Sorting for these things not only keeps you engaged, but also makes it easier to create a map once you've finished the relevant parts of the book.

When reading, it is helpful to take regular breaks. Many studies show that when you read continuously for extended periods of time, your attention, retention, and comprehension drop steadily. The longer you read in one sitting, the less your mind can process and remember the information. Therefore, when reading material of longer length, take short breaks in between.

The length of the breaks and how often you take them varies from person to person. A good standard to follow is to take a 5 to 10 minute break for every 20 to 25 minutes you spend reading. Again, this is not a hard and fast rule. You may find that a break every chapter or every page of notes may work better. Either way, make sure to take breaks. It will help you better understand and recall what you are reading. This is one of those areas where doing less is more.

A good way to fill up your time during breaks is to plan out your map. While you step away, you can assess the best way to organize the material you just read and the best place to put it on your map. During the break, you can even reexamine the text to ensure your comprehension is clear. In this way, while your brain is recharging, you are still active and productive with the material.

3. **Mind Map**

After previewing and reading the material, you can begin mind mapping. As always, you start in the center. You can start either with the title of the book, article, or chapter in the center or with a keyword that best sums up the idea.

From here you create the subtopics. You can supply subtopics in a few different ways. If you are mind mapping a non-fiction book, you can carry over the structure from the table of content or outline. This is an easy approach as you would simply use the chapter or title headings from the outline.

If no table of contents or outline is available, then you would pick the major points from the text. For instance, the major points of an astronomy book might include *Stars*, *Black Holes*, and *Galaxies*. You would set these items as your subtopics. Each point that the author makes would be a separate subtopic and hence represented by a distinct branch.

Within each subtopic, you build out the lower-level topics. If the table of contents or outline provides subheadings, you may use them as the subsets of your mind map. Again, if you are not following an outline or no subheadings exist, then pick out items from the text that would serve as good lower-level branches. In the example of mind mapping an astronomy book, under the subtopic of Stars, you might include, *types of stars*, *how stars form*, and *mass and energy of stars*. Descriptions, examples, instructions, supporting evidence, and arguments can all serve as effective lower-level topics. Then repeat this step, creating lower and lower branches, until you have noted all the pertinent information.

These are some things to consider when creating and filling in branches. Other things to consider might include material that you find difficult or are new and unfamiliar. You might also consider things you feel to be important and noteworthy. This would of course include items marked in bold or italics (if they weren't important, the author would not have taken the time to make the distinction).

Whether you include these things in subtopics or their subsets depends on the material as well as how you decide to arrange your map.

These are guidelines for non-fiction texts. Stories and novels require a different approach. Instead of using the main points of the author, you would use the literary elements that make up the story. You will learn more about this in chapter 7, but literary elements of a story or novel include things like plot, character, setting, and style. Using these familiar elements helps to organize your thoughts and overview according to how the story or novel is structured. In this way, your final mind map will include subtopics related to what the plot is, who the characters are, and where and when the story takes place. It can also include your opinions on such items as the strength of the storyline, the writing style of the author, and the development of the characters. This approach works well when mind mapping text of a fictional nature.

Now, if you feel confused about how to approach the mind map, it may mean that you do not fully understand what you read. Consequently, you may need to go back and read the text again. If this is the case, go ahead and do so. Don't feel that rereading is a waste of time. Often you have to read something a few times to process it fully. In these instances, think of each read as an additional preview you needed to forge a foundation strong enough to understand the material.

4. Review

After you create your mind map, the final step is to review. Reviewing involves comparing your mind map to the material you just finished reading. At this stage, you ensure your map accurately represents the content in the book, article, or report.

To do this, make sure you have noted all the pertinent information. Also, verify that all your hierarchies have been organized correctly. Determine whether your main branch should be a subset of another branch or if a subset should really be its own standalone branch. Often it makes sense to consolidate two branches into one or separate out one branch into multiple parts.

In your review, you may find that you need to redo your mind map completely. After examining the information, you may feel that your map could benefit from an entirely different approach. If so, by all means, do that. Learning is not linear. It can take a few back and forth to fully grasp a subject. So it may take you a few back and forth to get your mind map right. The process you go through to get it right is often what is required for your brain to grasp a subject fully. As in rereading, don't feel as though you are being inefficient or that you are wasting valuable time. It is simply what you needed to fully understand the information.

These are the steps to mind map written material. You start with preview, which gives you a foundation. Then you read while thinking about how the information can best be organized into a mind map. After reading, you build your map. Finally you review to ensure everything is correct. (If you are familiar with the SQ3R Reading Method, you will find it is a similar concept. The main difference is that these steps incorporate mind maps).

To see an example of this process in action, let's consider how you might use mind mapping to summarize this chapter. You'd start with a preview by reading the first few paragraphs of the introduction and conclusion. Then you would skim through the chapter scanning for important information.

As you scan, notice the items in bold and italics. In addition to the items in bold, this chapter has the following four items in italics: Articles and Reports, Books and Manuals, Textbooks, and Stories & Novels. Take note of these words as something important to know and understand. If you want, you might even read the first sentence following each one of these words. Since this chapter is on how to take notes of books using mind maps, you might deduce that these bolded items provide mind mapping instructions specific to these types of reading materials, giving you a better understanding of the content in this chapter.

This chapter has a few illustrations, so take a moment and briefly glance over each one. If these illustrations had comments next to them, you would read them. The illustrations in this chapter do not, so merely look over the pictures. At this point, if the content and/or illustrations you are previewing make little to no sense, don't worry. You are simply trying to expose yourself to the material.

After you preview, the next step is to read. As mentioned earlier, you read as you have in the past. You start at the introduction and move from one page to the next until you reach the conclusion. In this stage, many people have the tendency to disregard and pass over areas they explored during the preview step. Don't skip these materials. As we touched on briefly, repetition is important for memory and learning. The more you repeat a piece of information, the easier it becomes for your mind to process and recall. So although you read the introduction and glanced over other text and illustrations during the preview step, when you come across these items when reading, go over them again.

While reading, think about the key ideas and different points the chapter makes. In this example, the chapter first touches on the advantages of using mind maps to take notes of books. Further down, it lists the four steps to apply the technique: *Preview, Read, Mind Map, and Review.* Within each step, the chapter discusses what to do, what not to do, and important things to consider. These are all points the chapter makes, so keep a mental note of them.

As you pick out the main points, see if you can summarize them into keywords. For example, the intro discusses the advantages of using mind maps. The main advantage the chapter mentions is that mind maps allow you to be active with the material you are reading, so you can sum up this point with the keywords *Active with Material, Read*

Actively, or simply *Active*. As another example, under the *Read* step, a paragraph discusses the importance of taking breaks while reading material of longer length. This paragraph can be summed up with the keyword *Take Regular Breaks* or *Take Breaks*. Summarizing concepts into keywords does not have to be complicated. Simply find a word or a few words that effectively encapsulate a given concept.

After reading the text, you are ready to transcribe the information into a mind map. As you learned, you could approach this a couple ways. One, you can take the straightforward approach and follow the table of contents or outline. The outline of this chapter is fairly simple. There is an introduction, four mind map steps, and a conclusion. You would set these items as your subtopics or first level branches. It will look as follows:

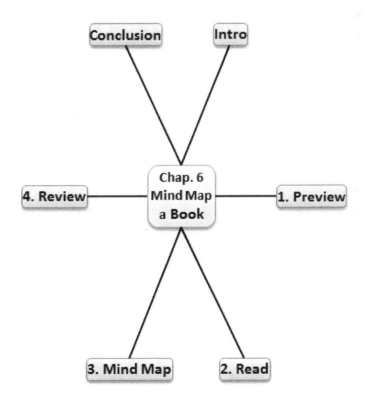

You may recall from the Preview step that instructions are further broken down by the type and length of material—*Articles and Reports, Books and Manuals, Textbooks,* and *Stories and Novels.* You can take this sub-section and add it as a subset of the Preview branch this way:

After developing this starting point for your mind map, you would gather details from each section and put them in their respective place. Considering our discussion above, the end result is a map that may look like this:

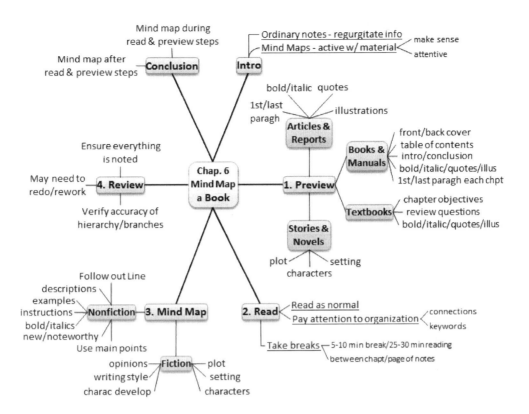

Looking at the image above, in the *Intro* branch, we recorded that ordinary notes regurgitate information whereas mind maps allow you to be active with the material, which helps in both comprehension and attention. Around the *Preview* branch, we listed the items to consider when previewing the four different types of materials. In the *Read* branch, we noted the importance of taking breaks as well as paying attention to the organization, specifically connections and keywords. The *Mind Map* branch broke out the instructions between fiction and nonfiction. For the *Review* branch, we included the important reminders that were outlined. Last, we included the point about the ordering of the steps in the *Conclusion* branch. This is one approach to mind mapping this chapter.

As you know, the other approach uses main points. Let's examine how to mind map this chapter using main points. The introduction discusses benefits, so one of the branches of our alternative map can be *Benefits*. The body of this chapter discusses the main steps, so the next branch can be *Mind Map Steps*. Throughout, the chapter provides valuable information on important things to consider. For this, you might set up a branch labeled *Important Considerations*. These items would represent your first-level branches, looking something like this:

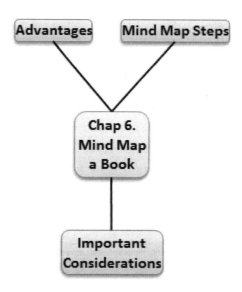

From here you would include specific details in the lower-level branches. For the *Benefit* branch, you would list the benefits that are discussed. Within the *Mind Map Steps* branch, you would list the instructions this chapter sets forth for each step. In the *Important Considerations* branch, you would list all the noteworthy issues and concerns that are addressed. It may look as follows:

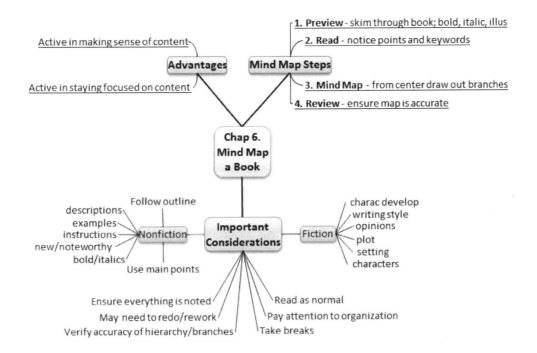

This is how you would go through the four steps to mind map this chapter. Now, you do not necessarily have to follow these steps in this order. If you wanted, you could start mind mapping in both the preview and reading stages. Previewing should give you a good awareness of what you are about to read. Even if your understanding is vague at that early stage, you should be able to pick out some of the subtopics and their subsets. Therefore, you could potentially sketch out a rough outline of the main hierarchies. This would be your starting point.

Then as you are reading, you can fill in the map with noteworthy information. While you read, you will come to natural stopping points. These may include the end of a chapter, a chapter section, or scene. When you come to these stopping points, you could take a minute to consider what the author said, fill in your map with the appropriate details, and then move forward to the next piece of text. To reiterate, you do not have to finish reading everything first before you start mind mapping. You can read and mind map simultaneously.

Whether you mind map while reading or after reading will depend on what you feel most comfortable doing. If you enjoy taking notes while reading, then map as you read. Otherwise, wait until you finish the material to begin. This will give you more time to collect your thoughts. Do what feels right for you.

Often, what feels right will depend on the length of the material you are mapping. For articles and reports, it might not make sense to stop frequently. For such short pieces, it will be best to read through the entry before starting the mind map. For longer works like books and novels, you will want to mind map as you are reading, especially by building lists of keywords as you go. This way you can note down the pertinent information while it is fresh in your mind.

This is how to mind map written works such as books and articles. Next we discuss how to use mind maps to take notes of lectures and presentations.

CHAPTER 4 - LECTURES AND PRESENTATIONS

When attending lectures, whether for school, work, or seminar, it is important to take notes. Studies show people who take notes during a presentation retain information longer and understand it better than those who simply listen. The simple act of writing down what the speaker is saying helps you to pay attention and process the information.

However, writing down notes the traditional way can make it hard to keep up. If you can keep up, it becomes an exercise in transcription rather than making sense of the presenter. You may find yourself writing and writing without a decent understanding of what he or she is saying. Alternatively, mind mapping allows you to focus more on comprehending the speaker and making relationships to the ideas that are being presented.

Mind mapping information delivered through a presentation is different from mapping information delivered through other means. You cannot pause a presentation if it is moving too fast or if you need time to collect your thoughts. Nor can you rewind it to go back to relevant points you may have missed. Therefore your thoughts, notes, and writing have to keep up with the pace of the person delivering the information. This requires that you simultaneously listen, watch, comprehend, and write down what is thrown at you. As difficult as this can be at times, mind maps can ease the process.

To mind map a lecture, start with the topic of the lecture in the middle of the page. Sometimes the lecturer makes it clear at the start what is going to be discussed. Note this down as the main topic.

Next, listen for subtopics. You may hear them at one of two places in the lecture. First, a lecturer may start off with a summary of his information. For instance, a speaker may start a lecture on the Roman Empire by saying *Today, we are going to cover the rise, height, and fall of the Roman Empire.* In this case, the subtopics of the lecture (and your mind map) would be *Rise of the Roman Empire, Height of the Roman Empire*, and *Fall of the Roman Empire*—though you may shorten that to *Rise, Height,* and *Fall* since your main topic would probably already be *The Roman Empire.*

You may also find subtopics in a lecture at verbal signposts. The lecturer may use verbal signposts such as *I will now discuss . . .* or *Moving to the next point . . . .* These are indications of a change in thought, likely requiring a new branch or subtopic. Other signposts to listen for are phrases like *On the other hand* or *Contrary to . . . .* These signposts also represent a possible change in thought and hence a potential new subtopic.

As the lecturer continues talking, use the graphic format that we illustrated earlier to note each detail as lower-level topics. Listen to the lecturer and pay attention to key points or information. Continue using branches to write down the important parts of the lecture or the concepts you want to remember. Don't forget to sketch out any interesting charts or visual aids.

At any point in the lecture, you can supplement the speaker by adding your own knowledge or realization about the subject. Don't think that the contents of your map have to be limited to the contents of the speech. Feel free to include insights that crop up as you listen in the course of the study or work session. The advantage of this note-taking method is that it is tailored to the needs of every person since each person has a unique way of making sense of new ideas and concepts. Adding personal insights as you listen can reinforce your memory and help you better comprehend what a speaker is saying.

If possible, you should prepare the main branches of your mind map before the start of the presentation or lecture. More often than not, your teacher or speaker will provide you with an outline summarizing the important points of a lecture to help you follow along. This can be a good starting point for your mind map. Preview the outline beforehand to familiarize yourself with what will be discussed. Then set up your map in accordance with the outline. As the speaker covers each area, fill in the map with the important details that are discussed.

To demonstrate, if you are given the following outline for a lecture on the Roman Empire, you can set up your mind map as follows.

Roman Empire
  I.   Rise of the Empire
        a. Augustus
        b. Conquests
        c. Frontiers of the Empire
 II.   Height of the Empire
        a. Political Reform
        b. Architecture
        c. Literature
        d. Social Change
III.   Fall of the Empire
        a. Economic Reasons
        b. Military Reason
        c. Political Reasons

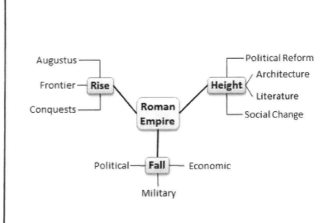

In the above example, the title of the outline represents the main idea of the lecture. Therefore it is placed in the center. The first indentation—*Rise*, *Height*, and *Fall* of the Empire—represent the subtopics of the main idea, so they are drawn radially around the main idea. The second indentation lists what will be discussed within each subtopic, so these items are drawn radially around them. This would be the entry point for your lecture. As the speaker covers each item, you would write down the important points discussed within the appropriate hierarchy or branch.

It's important to note that many times the speaker will be talking about more than just one main thought or idea. He or she may cover many topics that may be unrelated to each other. From the above example, you may be attending a lecture that discusses not only the Roman Empire, but the Persian and Han empires as well. Discussion of many unrelated topics is especially true if you are attending a long class or a daylong seminar going over a variety of information.

For lectures like these, with each new idea or topic discussed, you may opt to start with a new page. In our example, you may choose to use one page to note the Roman Empire, a separate page for the Persian Empire, and yet another page to record the history of the Han Empire. With each page, you will write the main idea in the center and build out the mind map. This will prevent confusion by keeping information within main topics separate from each other.

Furthermore, in the beginning, you may need practice before you are comfortable using mind maps in a live setting. If this is the case, stick with traditional note taking. Then after the lecture is over, summarize your notes into a mind map. Not only will this give you more practice with the technique, it will give you opportunity for repetition of the information, which will solidify your learning and put it into long-term memory.

With that said, don't put too much effort in trying to create the perfect mind map during the lecture. It is hard to predict exactly what information is going be presented and the direction the speaker will go with each branch. Simply focus on the points the speaker is trying to make and how they relate to each other. You can wait until after the lecture to review your map.

After the lecture, do in fact review your mind map. When you review, read over each fact and check that it is under the correct subtopic. It is an easy mistake to make and much simpler to fix with the lecture fresh in your mind, than hours or days later. Also while reviewing, take the time to think over the lecture to see if you can recall important information you may have missed. If additional details come up, add them now. Additionally, it can help to compare notes with another attendee. This way you can catch important points that you may have slipped by you.

If you feel it necessary, you can make a clean copy of your map. During the lecture you may have used abbreviations and short hand, your handwriting may have been rushed and messy, or you may not have been able to put as much detail in sketches of charts and diagrams as you would have preferred. Now is your chance to fix these things. Copy over your mind map and make the changes and corrections you see fit.

This is how to mind map information from a lecture or presentation. It is not too difficult if you take the right approach. You write the main topic of the lecture in the middle of the page. Then you listen for changes in thought to identify your subtopics. From there you record the essential facts and assertions into lower and lower topics. After the lecture or presentation, you review your map to ensure you have noted everything.

In the next section, we discuss other uses and applications of mind maps.

SECTION III

OTHER USES OF MIND MAPS

In the previous section, we examined note taking, the most common use for mind maps and the main reason it was created. The technique, however, is also useful in other life activities and practices. In this section, you'll discover these other activities, which include research, brainstorming, writing, planning, goal setting, and more.

Now, in order to apply mind maps in these activities effectively, it helps to know a little bit about the activity. For instance, to use mind maps for brainstorming or writing, it helps to have some basic knowledge about effective brainstorm techniques or the correct way to write. Otherwise, the instructions will make little sense and provide even less value. Therefore, we will not only show you how to use mind maps with these activities, but we will also talk a little bit about the activities themselves.

With that said, the chapters in this section will spend some time discussing the fundamentals of good research, writing, planning, etc. As a result, if you find that some of the discussions are too elementary or common sense, please be patient. Explaining the fundamentals is necessary to make the instructions on using mind maps easier to understand and more useful. Don't skim or skip the discussion, as it will still be valuable. We hope that after reading the following chapters, you will come out a better researcher, writer, planner, and facilitator of information.

CHAPTER 5 - RESEARCH

Research is the process of collecting information on a specific topic or subject. It involves gathering facts and data to discover, understand, or interpret an idea or concept. Over the course of your educational and professional career, you will be asked to perform a variety of research. In school, your teacher may ask you to perform research for a paper. At work, you may need to prepare for a proposal. Even in your personal life, you may have to research for a major purchase like a car or home.

Performing research can be a daunting task. It can be hard to know what to seek or even where to begin. That is because when you research, you are not familiar with the subject, which is the reason you are performing the task in the first place. Since you are not familiar with the subject, in a sense, you don't know what you don't know. You don't know what is available, what is useful, or what maybe important. As a result, it can be difficult to *know* where and/or how to begin.

Since mind maps are a great tool for arranging disjointed pieces of information into a coherent and organized way, they are a great tool to aid in this endeavor. With this system, you can take facts and data from a variety of sources and bring them together in a way that makes sense to both you and others.

Mind Maps aid research in two ways. First, they help you figure out from where to gather information. There are many places where you can acquire information. You can gather it from books, articles, encyclopedias, journals, magazines, interviews, internet, blogs, videos, etc. Mind maps help you narrow in on and select the best options for you and the type of research you are performing.

Second, mind maps help you assemble and arrange the information. Once you determine what sources you will use, you can take the information in these sources and use mind maps to organize them in a way to make meaningful sense. This process can help you understand concepts so you can develop concrete conclusions out of the data.

Gathering Information

As you learned, gathering information involves going out and identifying different sources to collect data. Since the potential number of sources can be overwhelming, it can help to set up a mind map of your available options. This will give you a bird's eye view of all your choices in one place. Below is an example of how this might look.

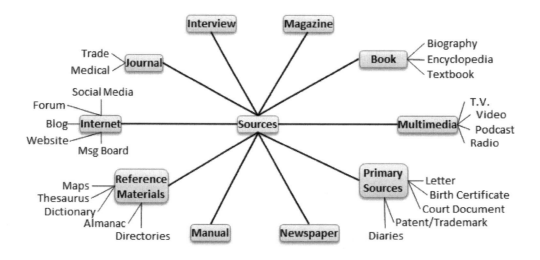

As you can see, this image neatly organizes all the possible sources for collecting information. The main branches include *Magazine, Book, Multimedia, Primary Sources, Newspaper, Manual, Reference Materials, Internet, Journal,* and *Interview.* Some of the main branches have sub-branches that list more specific materials. For example, the *Reference* branch specifies various types of reference sources like *Dictionaries, Thesaurus,* and *Almanacs.* With one glance, it is very clear to see your options and the subset of those options.

Since this map neatly lays out all of the possible places you may find information, it is a good starting point for any research you need to perform. When you have a study or question to explore, refer to this template. You will get a quick sense of the wide variety of the available options.

From here you can decide which avenues are best suited to your needs and most appropriate for your intended purposes. If your history teacher gives you an assignment to research the presidency of Franklin D. Roosevelt, the 32nd president of the United States, fitting resources for gathering such information would include textbooks, biographies and the encyclopedia. These materials specialize in content of such historical nature.

If however you are exploring more current topics such as marketing trends, then textbooks and encyclopedias will not be as suitable. Works like these take quite a long time to be published, so the information may be outdated by the time these publications reach circulation. For current trends, you might use the internet, blogs, podcasts, or even social media outlets like Facebook and Twitter. These avenues are a hotspot for trending news.

On the opposite spectrum, you have professional and scientific research. With this type, you might consider medical journals and other technical magazines and publications. Here, it might be wise to stay away from social media outlets. If you are writing a medical piece, readers are not likely to find you credible if you cite passages from random Facebook and Twitter posts.

Once you identify the type of sources you will use, you then focus on specific material within those sources. For example, if you decide to do part of your information gathering online, you will have many options as the Internet is very vast. Therefore you will want to identify specific sites on the net recognized as reliable resources for that information. If you are going to use books, you will need to identify the types of books that deal with the subject matter as well as specific titles and authors who are authorities on the topic.

For research on Franklin D. Roosevelt, for instance, some reliable website options might include Wikipedia, the free online encyclopedia, or FDRlibrary.marist.edu, a web resource for documents and other media about the President. As far as books, you might consider biographies about the president. Two popular biographies include *FDR,* by Jean Edward Smith, and *Traitor to His Class: The Privileged Life and Radical Presidency of Franklin Delano Roosevelt,* by H. W. Brands. Now you have precise material that discusses the information you are researching.

This goes without saying, but make sure to use only trustworthy sources and always double check your facts. The world is full of information, but not all of it is valid, useful, or accurate. For example, the website PresidentsUsa.net lists Roosevelt as the 31st president. This is clearly wrong. What is scary is that when searching for the term *Franklin Roosevelt*, this site comes up on the first page of the search engine results. Again, be cautious of where you get your information and always verify its accuracy.

As you think about suitable sources and narrow in on specific materials within those sources, you might build a new map to record your choices. Continuing with the example of the 32nd President, you might create a mind map that looks something like this.

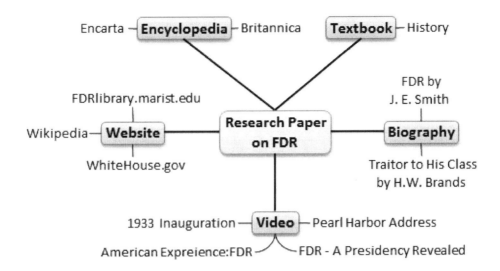

In the middle of the map we wrote *Research Paper on FDR Presidency*, as this is our central theme. From there we added branches for potential sources we can gather information about the president: *encyclopedia, textbook, biography, video,* and *website.* Within each branch, we specified the precise materials. In the website branch, we noted the following sites: *Wikipedia, FDRlibrary.marist.edu,* and *WhiteHouse.gov.* For books, we first narrowed in on the types of books: *textbooks, biographies,* and *encyclopedias.* Then within each type, we determined the exact books. As for video, we listed two of his popular speeches, *the 1933 Inauguration,* where he delivered his famous quote *the only thing we have to fear is fear itself,* and *the Pearl Harbor Address,* in which he delivered another famous quote, *a date that will live in infamy.* Under video, we also included couple of his documentaries, *FDR—A Presidency Revealed* and *American Experience: FDR.* With this mind map, we now have a starting point for our research.

This is first stage of research—gathering information. See how mind maps have helped you nicely narrow in on from where to gather data. Next time you are asked to examine a subject and are lost about where and how to start, start here. Begin from the mind map template with all of your potential options. From the template, pick out the sources that will have the information for which you are searching. After you gather the information, you can assemble it, which brings us to the next step.

Assembling Information

After you gather your books and articles, it is time to put together the information into a meaningful way. This starts with preview. As you learned in chapter 3, previewing gives you a sense of what is covered, so it will help you decide early on whether the material is worth putting the time and effort to go through. Previewing also helps you pinpoint the exact location where the information you seek resides. For example, if you are researching the presidency of Roosevelt, you don't have to read his entire biography to get that information. You simply focus on the chapters which discuss his presidency. The preview step will aid you in locating those chapters.

After preview, go through the content. This means diving into the materials you gathered. If you identified books and articles, read those texts. If you selected radio broadcasts, listen to the audio. If you chose documentaries, watch the videos. Dive into all the sources you identified.

As you dive in, take note of references to other sources they mention. For instance, if you are reading an article, you might come across a citation or recommendation to a book or other publication with additional information. You might consider looking into this book or publication as it may contain valuable facts essential to your research.

Finally, assimilate the content using mind maps. You can do this in one of two ways. You can create mind maps of each source and then bring them together into one large map. Riding on the Franklin Roosevelt example, you would create one mind map using the information in Wikipedia, another mind map using the information in his biography, and yet another from his documentary. Once you have these individual mind maps, you would merge the data from each diagram to make one giant diagram that encompasses the entire research. With this method, you begin with many small maps and end with a single large one.

The other approach is to simply start with a single large map. You would first read all the sources. Then you would analyze the content. From there, you would organize the information into a mind map. In this approach, you begin and end with one map.

The option you choose will depend on the extent of your research. If your research is involved, the first option might work most effectively. Reading over several lengthy books and journals may prove difficult to remember by the time you start mind mapping. However, if your research is relatively brief, you might want to go with the second option. You will be able to read through all the information at once, as if it were one single source. Then you would put the mind map together with what you learned.

Whichever option you choose, you will need to determine how you will define the branches. One way to do this is to look at where information is repeated. If in your research, you notice multiple sources talking about the same information, this might be important to note and worth creating a unique branch. For example, reading about FDR, you will encounter the New Deal. The New Deal was a series of economic programs FDR implemented in response to the Great Depression. The New Deal was a big deal during Roosevelt's presidency, so every source from encyclopedias to biographies will discuss it. Another topic multiple sources will discuss is World War II. Roosevelt served as president during the war and was instrumental in leading the military alliance that defeated Nazi Germany, Italy, and the Empire of Japan. As a result, these two would be important enough to set as main branches. Seeing similarities from different sources can help you define a branch.

Then with sub-branches, you can list what each source says about the branch. With the New Deal, one source may focus on what historians call the 3 *R's*, Relief, Recovery, and Reform. Another source might mention the specific programs that were created, like Social Security, Federal Deposit Insurance Corporation (FDIC), Securities and Exchange Commission (SEC) and the Housing Authority. Still a different source may discuss the increased federal regulation of the economy. So now you have different sources supplying the lower-level branches that support the main branch or subtopic.

Ironically, another way to define branches is to notice where there are differences. You can do this by looking at what one source says that another does not. One source may criticize the former president's policies and decisions, while another might support them. So now you have two additional branches, one titled *Criticism* and another titled *Support*. Within the branches, you can include the arguments each source lists.

An alternative way to identify differences is to look at how the topic you are researching varies from other similar topics. In this example, you might look at what sets President Roosevelt apart from other presidents. A major distinction is that FDR had polio, which took away his ability to walk. Essentially, he was confined to a wheel chair during parts of his presidency. Also, he was the only U.S. President to serve 4 terms. You can list these as unique branches on your map. Then with the use of lower-level branches, you can detail the specific aspects of these unique characteristics.

Considering the above discussion, this is how a mind map of Franklin Roosevelt might come together.

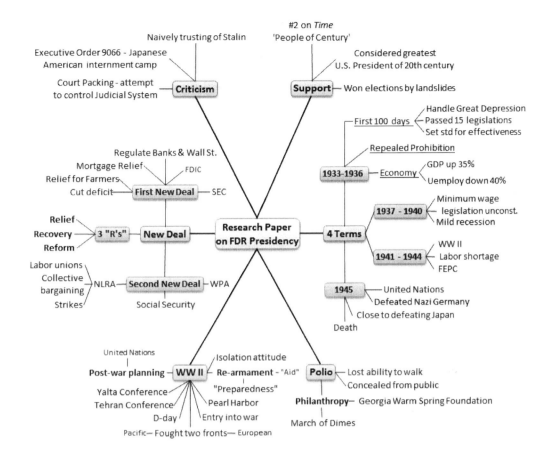

At initial glance this map looks messy and disorganized. If you take a moment to examine the details, however, you'll see the information is fairly neat and organized. Let's go through the details together. Based on our discussion, we started with *New Deal*, *World War II*, *Criticism*, *Support*, *4 Terms*, and *Polio* as the subtopics or first level branches.

Within the *4-Terms* branch, we added sub-branches for each term. Then within each sub-branch, we listed noteworthy information that occurred in that term. For example, in FDR's first term, which spanned from 1933-1936, he vigorously worked to manage the Great Depression. During the first 100 days of that term, he worked with Congress around the clock and passed 15 legislations. This set a benchmark for effectiveness to which all subsequent presidents are compared. To generate revenue, he repealed the ban on alcohol. As a result of his combined efforts, in his first term GDP rose by 35% and employment fell almost 40%. As you see, these are all noted in the map.

Under the *New Deal* branch, we also added sub-branches. We mentioned earlier that the New Deal focused on the *3R's*, so we set that as one branch. Since the New Deal came in two phases, which historians call the First New Deal and the Second New Deal, we set them as sub-branches as well, with the specific programs that were created in each phase as subsets.

For the *Criticism* and *Support* branches, we included the fine points of people's approval and disapproval of Roosevelt. He was widely criticized for naively trusting Joseph Stalin, the leader of the Soviet Union with whom Roosevelt worked closely to defeat Germany. On the opposite end, he was considered by many to be the greatest president of the 20th century, coming in second place on Time Magazine's coveted *People of the Century*. Again, all of these items are noted on the map.

With the *WW II* branch, we listed chronologically (from right to left) the events that transpired. Initially, most Americans took an isolationist stance and did not want to be involved in the War. This attitude shifted to rearmament, providing *aid* to allies and *preparing* for a possible conflict. After the attack on Pearl Harbor, FDR entered the US into war, fighting on both the European and Pacific fronts. Noteworthy events included D-day, Tehran Conference, and the Yalta Conference. As Roosevelt brought the war to a close, he pushed to create a world democracy, or the United Nations.

In the *Polio* branch, we filled it with interesting facts about his struggle with the disease. Not only did Roosevelt lose his ability to walk, but he concealed it or did his best to conceal it from the public. There are only two know photos of him in a wheel chair. He also helped to find a cure for the disease. In one initiative, Roosevelt asked the public to send in dimes to help fund research. The initiative became known as the March of Dimes. After accomplishing its initial goal of eliminating polio, March of Dimes became a non-for-profit organization that currently works to improve the health of mothers and babies.

The events surrounding Roosevelt's presidency is quite interesting. What is more interesting is how well mind maps summarize them. With only about half a page, we are able to list not only what occurred, but with great detail. This is the amazing power of mind mapping.

Here you learned how to use mind maps to take different ideas and information from research and bring them together in a structured and coherent way. In the next chapter you will learn to do the opposite. You will learn how to use mind maps to start from nothing, and through brainstorming, bring forth valuable ideas and solutions.

CHAPTER 6 - BRAINSTORMING

Brainstorming is a creativity technique that involves generating unique and original solutions to problems. With this technique, you break away from conventional thinking to look at circumstances in new ways. This helps you overcome mental road blocks to reach better ideas and solutions.

When it comes to brainstorming, ideas and solutions rarely appear out of nowhere. They require work to bring them to fruition. More importantly, when an idea comes into fruition, it rarely comes in a complete and ready-to-use state. Often it needs to be tweaked and massaged until it is just right. This is the nature of brainstorming.

Due to this nature, the brainstorming process can be broken into two steps. The first step is to get all of your thoughts about a topic or problem out of your head. The objective is that some of these thoughts can be crafted into ideas and solutions for which you are looking. In fact, you want to accumulate as much of your thinking as possible on the topic you are brainstorming. The more you collect, the more ideas you can develop. The more ideas you can develop, the greater your chances of finding one that will fit your need.

The second step is to take the thoughts you come up with and develop them into workable ideas and solutions. This is where mind maps come into play. After accumulating your thoughts, you use mind mapping to *tweak* and *massage* them. You cross out things that won't work, highlight insights that will, bring together similar concepts, and separate out dissimilar ones. You continue working until you start forming useful ideas.

This is the essence of brainstorming with mind maps. You start with quantity and work your way to quality. This chapter will guide you through both. It will start by presenting an easy technique to help get your thoughts out of your head and onto paper. Then, it will show you how to lasso those thoughts to formulate worthwhile ideas and solutions.

Collecting Your Thoughts

In order to collect your thoughts effectively, it helps first to understand another principle of your mind. In this book's intro, you learned about the associative nature of your brain. In regard to this, you learned that anytime you hear something new, your brain likes to connect it to something old. Thus everything you know is linked together. Your thoughts are not floating freely around in your mind, but instead are anchored to one another like the roots of redwood trees.

This also means your thoughts activate or elicit each other. That is, anytime you think of something, your mind brings to consciousness other thoughts to which they are connected. For example, when you look at an old picture, what normally happens? Your mind elicits memories of the time the picture was taken. It recounts the past in exquisite detail from what you were doing, where you were living, and the people you were around. These memories then activate other memories, for instance goals you wanted to accomplish and how you felt during those times. All this occurs simply from glancing at a photo of a moment in time.

The same process occurs with other types of thoughts. When you hear the word *math*, in a flash you probably think about addition and subtraction. You may even conjecture up an image of the multiplication table you were taught in school. If you have difficulty with math, the word probably brings up memories of your struggle with the subject. Since math deals with numbers, you may also think about other numbers in your life, such as your most recent cell-phone bill. This may trigger you to remember that the due date is approaching for this bill. As you see, thinking of a thought can flood your mind with other thoughts to which you have connected. If you've ever found yourself thinking about a completely off topic, and were baffled by how your mind strayed in that direction, this should shed some light.

You can use this principle to get your thoughts churning about a topic or problem. Since thinking of a thing triggers the recollection of other things, you start by thinking of a word or concept related to the topic you want to brainstorm. This will trigger many thoughts to come into your awareness. As these thoughts come up, you note them down. You want to note anything and everything that comes to mind.

Then you repeat the step. You look at each item that initially came up and see what additional thoughts and ideas those items trigger. You write those down as well. You keep doing this until you fill your paper with as many pieces of information as will fit. This is a quick and easy way to flesh out a collection of thoughts with which to work. As pointed out, only then can you develop useful ideas and solutions.

Let's see how this might look with an example. Suppose that you work for a prominent hotel chain. Your company just received the results of a customer satisfaction survey, and the response was overwhelmingly poor. As a result, your boss has asked you to come up with ways to improve the company's customer experience. So you go back to your office to do some serious brainstorming.

You start by writing the topic you want to brainstorm in the center of the page. Since you are looking for ways to improve customer satisfaction, your topic in this example can simply be *Improve Customer Satisfaction*. Now look at this topic and notice the different thoughts that come into your awareness. Some things that come to mind may include *relationship, loyalty, interaction, purchase, service*. These words are related to customer and satisfaction, so they are likely to conjure up when we think of customer satisfaction. As each thought emerges, jot it down.

During this process, avoid censoring your thoughts. The point of the exercise is to get as much material as possible out of your head and onto paper, so write down anything and everything that arises. Don't worry about spelling, punctuation, or grammar. Even include thoughts that are unrelated to the topic. For example, if you start thinking, *I don't want to do this task* or *I hate my boss for giving me this assignment*, still write it down. No matter how farfetched or ridiculous the thought, put it on paper.

In the initial run through, your page might look something like this:

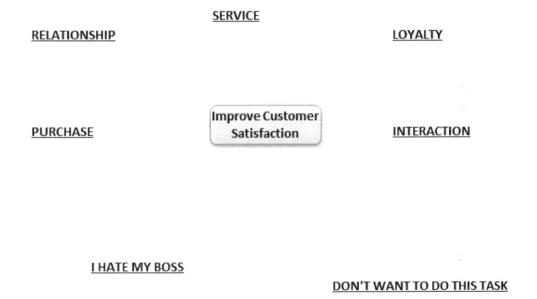

In the middle of the sheet, you have the main topic you are brainstorming. Around the main topic is the list of thoughts and concepts that thinking about the main topic brought to surface.

From here, you take the items that were brought to surface and allow each one to trigger its own set of thoughts and ideas. For example, you might start with the word *Relationship*. Looking at this word may cause you to think about the different relationships in your life, such as the ones with your friends, family, spouse, employees, etc. So you would write them down.

Then you might move on to the statement, *I don't want to do this task.* This will likely trigger you to think about all the things that you would rather be doing instead of this assignment. Activities that may come to mind may include golfing, eating at your favorite restaurant, or spending time with your spouse or friends.

Next you might look at the statement, *I hate my boss for giving me this assignment.* Your initial reaction might be, *I sure hope he doesn't see this or I'll be in big trouble.* Afterwards you might think about why you hate your boss or the other things that you hate in your life. Record everything. Continue this for the rest of the items.

Once you complete this for the first set of thoughts, do this for the second set. In the above example, one of the terms that came up in the first go around was *Relationship*, and this term triggered *Family*, *Friends*, *Spouse*, and *Employee*. Again, you would take the second set of terms and have each one trigger its own series of phrases. Thinking of *family* might make you realize that you don't *spend enough time with them.* Thinking of *spouse* might make you realize that your *anniversary* is coming up soon. Again, log everything. Repeat this for the remaining items in the second set. At this stage, your page will look something like this:

anniversary
spouce
friends   employee   laundry   service industry   Earn Points
family   Free Upgrade

SERVICE   Reward Loyalty   Free Amenities

RELATIONSHIP   hospitality   Free Nights

spend more time with family   **LOYALTY** Dependable

Reliable

spending   Honest

hugs

money   **PURCHASE** | Improve Customer Satisfaction | **INTERACTION**   smile

contact

free wasted money   credit card   angry   mean   nice

save money   points   rude   courteous

cash

hassle to carry   have to drive to restaurnt

eating at Lobster World

I HATE MY BOSS   golfing

hate traffic   **DON'T WANT TO DO THIS TASK**   get out doors

Looking for parking sure hope boss doesn't see this

playing with my kids

waiting in line   watching game with buddies

waste time

dealing with people

In the center you have *Improve Customer Satisfaction*. Around that you have written *Relationship, Loyalty, Interaction, Purchase, Service, I dislike this task*, and *I hate my boss*. To make these items visually apparent, they are underlined and in bold. Within these items you have listed what each one triggered. As pointed out earlier, *Relationship* triggered *Friends, Family, Spouse, Employees*. Loyalty prompted *Reliable, Dependable*, and *Honest*. *I dislike this task* initiated other activities you'd rather be doing like *golfing, playing with my kids, eating at Lobster World*, etc. These items are in lower case bold, no underline. Within those items are other items and on and on.

Right now, as you can see, this sheet is fairly disorganized. It is full of scribbles and notes scrambled in all directions. This is o.k. In fact, this is more than o.k. This is the creative process. You first get all of your thoughts out of your head. Then you work through them to reveal ideas and solutions, which takes us to the next part of the process.

Developing Solutions

Once you get a set of thoughts about your subject or topic onto paper, you are ready to use mind maps. At this stage, you will evaluate your jumbled thoughts and lasso them into a rational, organized framework. Here, you can work backwards and forwards on ideas without the weight of a blank starting point. You can also take the words and terms you've put down and use them as a basis for the branches in your map.

In this stage, you can be more judgmental. You can identify items you like. You can cross out items you dislike. You can decide which items will work and which won't. Here, you can let out your inner critic.

This is how the process goes: Begin by glancing over everything you have written in the brainstorm sheet and see if anything jumps out as ideas and suggestions worth developing. For starters, you might look at the word *Relationship* and think that relationships are important to people. What if your hotel catered to maintaining and developing healthy relationships? This would surely improve your customer experience.

One thought the word relationship triggered is *Family*. To cater to relationships, maybe your hotel could be family focused. It could have an atmosphere where families could enjoy spending time with each other. Another thought that came up for us was *Spouse*. With this you might think about offering an experience couples might enjoy. This can include having a suite for couples or providing some sort of a romance package. Many hotels cater to marriages by holding wedding receptions, so this is something you might consider offering as well.

Next you might look at the things that you would rather be doing. This may get you thinking about leisure the hotel can offer that guests would enjoy. In your brainstorming session, you wrote that you would rather be eating at your favorite restaurant, golfing, or watching the game with your buddies. You can use these as worthy ideas. That is, it would be great to have a restaurant in your hotel where guests can gather and eat, and it might be nice to have a large screen T.V. in the lobby or waiting area where guests can relax or catch up on the news, weather, or sports. Although it will be difficult to offer a golf experience in-house, you could offer an outing to the local golf course. These things might get you thinking about other activities, tours, and excursions your hotel could provide that people would enjoy doing.

Then you might look at the things that you dislike or hate doing. Thinking about these inconveniences might make you reflect on inconveniences people experience when traveling or staying in hotels. Naturally, you would want to offer conveniences that make your customer's journey less of a hassle. Some conveniences could include providing shuttle service to and from the airport, informational handouts about the local attractions and events, easy check-in, etc.

As you start coming up with these ideas, you can put them in a mind map to explore. You would start with a fresh piece of paper, and in the center write the topic. Then you would take each idea or potential idea that looking at the brainstorm sheet brings to mind and branch out with a subtopic. You would branch out with as many subtopics as you can.

At this stage, your subtopics are only potential solutions. You still need to work out the details to determine their feasibility. You will do this with lower-level topics. In them, you would include things like how to achieve the idea, important things to consider, costs and benefits, potential problems and limitations, as well as a workable timeline to implement. Anything you need to work out, you can include as a lower-level topic.

Continuing with the hotel example, we start by writing *Improve Customer Experience* in the center. From the above discussion, the following were possible ideas that came up for us when we looked at the brainstorm sheet: *Family Friendly*, *Couples*, *Activities*, and *Conveniences*, so we branch out with them as follows:

This is our starting point. Since at the moment we have only potential solutions, each branch still needs to be fleshed out into lower-level topics. For this example, we will flesh out the *Family Friendly* branch.

Families generally want a place where children can have fun and parents can relax. They want a safe environment, and in some cases, facilities such as a swimming pool, game room, play area, or a kids' club. Also important on the list are sights and attractions to see and do with the children in the local area. Beaches, parks, and other outdoor activities are all key in getting the balance right on a family holiday. We place these items around the family-friendly branch. It will look something like this:

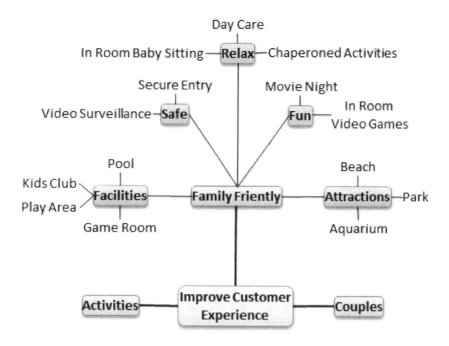

When we started with *Improve Customer Experience,* one idea to achieve that included making it *Family Friendly.* Within this subtopic, we developed as many details as we could about how to make the hotel enjoyable for families. We did this inside the subcategories of *Facilities, Safe, Relax, Fun,* and *Attractions.*

We can go one step further and analyze our ideas. We might decide that a pool could be too expensive to build and maintain, but a game room and play area would be more feasible. As for an aquarium and other attractions, we could work out deals with the local parks and other recreation companies to offer discounted entrance fees for the guests. As you analyze each idea, you would note them within the respective lower-levels.

You would do this for the remaining subtopics—*Couples, Activities,* and *Conveniences.* You would develop and work out solutions into lower and lower levels just as we did here.

As you do all of this, pay attention to and note any feelings and suggestions that come up. Sometimes an idea will surface, but it will surface with a feeling that it is too hard, has already been done, or is too demanding to implement. At other times when an idea emerges, it will emerge with suggestions. For example, you might think of something and simultaneously you will have thoughts like, *John in customer service knows a lot about this, maybe he can help me in this area*, *If I move forward here, I may have to cut my losses there*, or *This is a good plan, but it may not work in this context*. As feelings and suggestions emerge, note them under that branch.

In addition, be sure to scan all areas of the brainstorm sheet regularly. You may get an idea from one section of the sheet, but the details of how to develop and execute it might be located in an entirely different part. For example, the idea to eliminate inconveniences came from thinking about the different things you hate doing; however, there are also very useful suggestions for improving convenience under *Loyalty*, *Service*, and *Purchase*. These ideas you can pull directly from the brainstorm sheet without having to spend extra time to think them up on your own.

After working through these steps, you will have a mind map with many possible ideas and solutions. You can then go through each solution you pulled together to evaluate the one or ones that will serve your needs the best. This is how you brainstorm with mind maps. First you gather all of your thoughts on a topic, and then you bring them together in a coherent structure.

Additional Tips

Above we showed you one way to get your ideas on to paper—looking at a problem or thought and seeing what additional thoughts they trigger. This method is very effective in getting your mind flowing. It is especially effective with mind mapping because, like mind maps, it deals with keywords and ideas and expanding on those keywords and ideas. However, if you don't like this method, or for some reason it doesn't work for you, there are others methods you can employ.

One method that works well is called reverse brainstorming. With reverse brainstorming, instead of looking for ways to solve a problem, you look for ways to make it worse. Then you take the reverse of what you come up with as potential solutions.

Continuing with the hotel example, instead of thinking about how to improve customer satisfaction, you start by thinking of ways to lower it even more. The ideas that you come up with may include *be rude to customers*, *make the check-in process inconvenient*, *charge for amenities*, and *provide wrong directions and false information*. Then you take the reverse of these ideas. Reversing them would give you, *be polite*, *make check-in as convenient as possible*, *offer free amenities*, and give *accurate timely and advice*. Now you have positive ideas as a starting point. This is a very effective method for brainstorming.

This is my own quack psychology, but I think the reason this strategy works so well is because, for some reason, our mind does not like to give us what we want, especially when we want it. This is evidenced by the fact that our best replies in a conversation or interview come after they are over. Our best answers on an exam arise after we've handed it in. Our best remedies turn up when we no longer need them. I am sure you can attest to this. In the same way, our mind will more easily hand us ideas to exacerbate a problem than to solve it. With reverse brainstorming, you in a sense *trick* your mind into giving you effective and worthwhile solutions.

Another method to stir your thoughts is called starbursting. This method works by asking questions. You ask a host of probing queries about the problem and/or potential solutions. Possible questions you might ask can be anything from what is causing the problem to what are all the surrounding issues, what resources are available, who does the solution benefit, and how have others solved the problem? Once all the questions that come to mind are written down, you answer them as clearly as you can. Each answer can trigger a collection of additional questions. You repeat the question and answer until the topic has solidified into workable ideas.

Reverse brainstorming and starbursting are two additional ways to spark the creative juices. They can be applied individually or together. You might start with the method discussed in the beginning of this chapter. From there, you might move to the starburst method to answer critical questions. Finally, you can throw in reverse brainstorming with details that need additional inspiration. Play around with a combination that works most naturally for you.

It's useful to keep in mind that you don't necessarily have to get all of your thoughts out of your head before you start mind mapping. Brainstorming is a creativity exercise, which means you do not have to follow a structured pattern. If you start churning out ideas that you can push to a mind map, there is no reason why you should wait. Depending on the difficulty of the problem, you may have to go back and forth between the mind map and brainstorm sheet a few times.

Furthermore, when you are mapping out potential ideas and solutions, although we suggested starting with a clean sheet, this is not necessary. You can use the brainstorm sheet as a starting point for your mind map. The problem with the brainstorm sheet, as you saw in the illustration, is that it can quickly become disorganized and messy. If however you can ignore the messiness or your ideas come up in ways where you can easily connect lines and branches between sub and lower-level topics, feel free to turn the brainstorm sheet into a mind map.

Last, given the nature of brainstorming, you may not come up with useable ideas and solutions in the first attempt. As a result, you may have to develop a series of mind maps. In the first mind map, you might advance one set of ideas. Then you could go back to the brainstorm sheet to flesh out more thoughts, which you foster in subsequent maps. From there, you can combine the first, second, and third mind maps to craft the *ultimate* solution, one that is more complete and in-depth than any individual mind map could have produced.

Brainstorming and researching, of course, are two things you probably won't be doing for the fun of it. There will likely be some purpose behind them. You will probably be applying them to another task like writing or planning. In the subsequent chapters, you will learn how to use mind maps for these activities and more.

CHAPTER 7 - WRITING

Writing is an indispensable part of our lives. It is necessary when we put together a research paper for school, a proposal for work, or even an email to a friend. As important as writing is, however, it can be difficult. Many people find the task to be an overwhelming endeavor.

This is because writing is not objective like math or science, where you work out a formula or remember facts. Instead, it is qualitative and requires a certain degree of creativity. It requires that you come up with your own words to communicate what it is you want to say.

The problem doesn't go away with figuring out *what* to say. You still have to overcome the challenge of *how* to say it. Where should you begin? How should you present the content? When should you handle contradictions? All these matters add to the difficulty.

Mind maps can simplify these challenging aspects of writing. As an organizational tool that supports creative thinking, mind mapping can help you organize and bring structure to the otherwise messy and disorganized nature of creative thinking. It can assist you in figuring out what to say and how in the most efficient way possible.

Writing comes in two forms—non-fiction and fiction. Non-fiction is based on facts. It includes works that teach and communicate such as essays, guidebooks, textbooks, and technical manuals. This book, a guide on mind mapping, is work of non-fiction. Fiction, on the other hand, is a class of writing that is not based on facts. It comprises works of an imaginative nature such as stories, novels, poems, and fairytales.

The reason we are making the distinction is because writing non-fiction is very different from writing fiction. The literary elements used in fiction do not transfer over well to non-fiction. As a result, applying mind maps varies depending on what you are writing. In this chapter, you will learn how to use mind maps for both non-fiction and fiction. We begin with non-fiction.

Writing Non-Fiction

Using mind maps for non-fiction is fairly straightforward. Basically, you open with the thesis in the center, and then around it, you build out the points you want to discuss about the thesis. From there you list out the details that will support those points. Below, we provide a more comprehensive explanation that walks you step-by-step through the process.

1. Thesis—Start by identifying the thesis, the central topic, or key concept you are trying to convey to the reader. If your assignment is for school or work, your teacher or boss will often tell you what this will be. At other times, you will have to develop a topic on your own. In these cases, pick one you know a lot about or would enjoy learning. Once you have a thesis in mind, write it down in the center of the page. This will be the main topic of the mind map.

2. Points—After identifying the thesis, think through the points you want or need to discuss. What is it that you plan to communicate or are required to address about the topic? Your goal here is to come up with as many points as possible. Create a branch for each one. These will be the subtopics or first-level branches.

Often, figuring out the points can be difficult. You may not know what to include, let alone where to start. Fortunately, there are ways to come up with potential points. One approach is to think about your objective for the writing. Non-fiction works are written with a specific objective in mind. They are written either to explain, to persuade, or to describe. Most non-fiction works fall into one of these three categories. Below we define what these objectives are and what to consider as possible points and hence subtopics for your mind map.

• **To Explain**—Writings of this type are explanatory in nature. Their primary goal is to inform, educate, or deliver information about an issue, subject, method, or idea. Most academic works are of this form. When mapping explanatory pieces, set each piece of information or issue you want to explain as a branch.

• **To Persuade**—This type of writing focuses on arguing a point. The emphasis here is to influence your reader to think or act in a certain way. Examples of this type of writing include reviews, recommendations, and speeches. In persuasive papers, each argument or benefit you want the reader to consider can be represented by a unique branch. You can also create unique branches for counter arguments you would like to address.

• **To Describe**—These writings provide a description. The descriptions can be about a person, place, experience, object, or event. For the most part, anything you perceive or observe can be the focus of descriptive writing. When mind mapping, each item you want to describe about a topic can be a branch.

This is one way to help you come up with points for your writing. Another way is to look at the mode your writing will use to present the information. Non-fiction works use various modes to present content. Among the many options, the most popular modes compare and contrast, list advantages and disadvantages, illustrate cause and effect, or walk one through the steps of a process. We'll take a closer look at these modes to see how they too can help you develop your points for writing and subtopics for your mind map.

• **Compare & Contrast**—In using this mode, you show how two or more ideas are similar or different from each other. Comparing shows how they are similar, while contrasting shows how they differ. When using this mode, you can set each item of comparison or each item of distinction as a branch.

• **Advantage & Disadvantage**—The mode here looks at two opposing sides of a situation or outcome. It uses facts to weigh in on the positives and negatives. Each advantage or disadvantage you want to discuss can thus be represented by a point and branch in your mind map.

• **Cause and Effect**—This takes an event and looks at its cause, effect, or both. It focuses on why something happens (cause) and what happens as a result (effect). Each cause of a given outcome and each effect of a given cause can be a distinct point or branch.

• **Process**—This mode presents the steps required to perform a task or the sequence necessary for an event. It takes a task or event, and lists out the order—step 1, step 2, step 3 or first, second, third—that something happens or happened. Each step or sequence in the process can be identified as a branch.

Analyzing the objective and mode are a few ways to come up with the points for your writing. Your objective is your goal, and the mode is how you will achieve that goal. Although most non-fiction falls into three objectives, there are a lot of modes. We provided only four here as there is not enough room to discuss them all. To learn the other modes, please reference books on writing as they will cover this information more thoroughly.

One more suggestion is to think about the questions you want to answer for the readers or what the reader would want answered. Each question you want to address can be represented by a distinctive branch on the map.

3. Details—Once you have written the main thesis in the center and placed the points you want to discuss about the thesis as the subtopics, it is time to think about the details. In the context of non-fiction writing, by detail we mean, *what is it that you want to say about each point?* This will be the meat of your composition as your details will support the points, which in turn will support the thesis. You will place these items as lower-level topics on your map.

There are many ways to provide detail in writing. They can be provided by facts, descriptions, examples, definitions, opinions, or viewpoints. More or less, anything that will argue or reinforce a point can be a worthwhile detail. So for each subtopic in your mind map, create lower-level branches with details you will use to support it.

4. Evaluate—After you have plotted the thesis, points, and the details within each point, you should have a rough foundation for your writing. At this stage, you should go through and evaluate what you have mapped out. Analyze each branch and make sure the points and details you have listed make sense. In addition, make sure that they are appropriate for the assignment and that they help support the main thesis or topic for which you are writing. Any changes you need to make or thoughts you want to develop further, you can do so now.

There are additional things to consider during the evaluation. For one, pay attention to first-level branches to ensure they will convey what it is you want to convey about the thesis you have chosen or been assigned to write. Moreover, with these first-level branches, ensure that you have sufficient details in lower-level branches to develop them. Just as when mind mapping to take notes, determine if any of your main branches should really be a sub-branch. Vice versa, determine if you included details within a sub-branch that really ought to stand alone as a separate and unique branch. These are additional considerations when evaluating your map.

5. Narrow Your Options—Next, it is time to select the specific points and details you will discuss. Your goal when mapping out your writing is to bring forth as many sub and lower-level topics as possible. However, more than likely, you will not be able to use everything that you come up with. You will have to narrow your options.

When narrowing your options, think about the constraints you have, such as space and time. If you are restricted by page count, go with points and details that will not require a lot of words to explain. You can also choose the most important details or those that back up your claim the best. If you are restricted by time, select those that will require the least effort to explain. These are a few ways to help you narrow your options.

6. Identify Order—After you narrow your choices, think about the order you want to present those choices. Which point will you discuss first? Which one will you discuss second, and so on? Put a number next to each branch to signify their sequence. Below are some general guidelines for arranging information within a paper.

• **Simple to complex**—Talk about the simpler points first, and then move to the more complex ones.

• **First to last**—If you are writing about a process, talk about the beginning or initial steps before discussing the subsequent ones.

• **Shortest to longest**—Address concepts that can be articulated using fewer words before moving to ones that require a lengthy description.

This is the process of writing non-fiction using mind maps. You begin with the main *thesis* or topic in the center. Then you draw out subtopics that address the *points* you want to discuss about the thesis. From there, you draw lower-level topics that *detail* those points. After accomplishing this, you *evaluate*, *narrow*, and *identify* the order you want to discuss everything. When you finish these 6 steps, you will have your writing laid out, or in this case, mapped out.

With everything mapped out, you can begin writing. At this stage, all you have to do is convert your mind map into linear form. You will do this by going through and discussing each point or branch on your map in the order that you established.

If your assignment involves research, follow the instructions in chapter 5 on research. It will show you how to use mind maps to gather and collect information. In many cases, you can take the map you develop there to help you write the paper. Each subtopic in the research map can represent a point in your writing. In fact, the narrative we included about FDR at the end of that chapter was based on the research mind map we created. We went through each main branch and picked the details one-by-one to compose the narrative. This is how you can use research as a basis for your writing.

As with research, you can also use brainstorm mind maps as a basis for your writing. Following the instructions in chapter 6 on brainstorming, you can work out ideas for a thesis or topic and what you will discuss for that topic. The map you create from the session can thus serve as a guide for your writing. After you create the map, all you will need to do is *evaluate*, *narrow*, and *identify* the order you will introduce the information.

Paragraph Structure

The above is one way to apply mind maps to develop and organize works of non-fiction. Another way is to follow the building blocks of formal writing. Below we discuss these blocks and how to build them with mind maps.

The building block of all writing is the paragraph. A paragraph is a group of sentences that discusses one topic or idea. The idea can describe a place, character, process, or event. It can be used to explain a point or help develop a point. This is the fundamental nature of paragraphs.

In formal writing, each paragraph has three parts. The three parts are introductory sentence, body sentence, and concluding sentence. The introductory sentence presents the main idea. It tells you what the rest of the paragraph is going to be about. The body sentences are often called supporting sentences because they support the introductory sentence. They expand, describe, or prove the claim introductory sentences make. The concluding sentence reiterates the introductory sentence and summarizes the information in the body. Sometimes it is used to lead into the next paragraph. This is the basic structure of a paragraph.

To illustrate, let's use the above paragraph as an example. The first sentence, *In formal writing, each paragraph has three main parts*, is the introductory sentence. It sets the stage for what will be discussed, which is the three main parts of a paragraph. The next five sentences represent the body. They expand on the introductory sentence by describing each of the three parts. The last sentence, *This is the basic structure of a paragraph*, is the concluding sentence. It both summarizes the main point of the passage and concludes it. These are the formal guidelines our teachers taught us.

To create longer pieces, like articles, reports, and essays, you bring multiple paragraphs together. You bring them together the same way you do sentences, by combining introductory, body and concluding segments. The introductory paragraph introduces or grabs the attention of the reader. The body of this longer piece supports and expands on the introduction. Then the conclusion summarizes and ties together the main points of the piece, while bringing everything to close.

These are the fundamentals of good writing. You take introductory, supporting, and concluding sentences to form paragraphs. Then you take introductory, supporting, and concluding paragraphs to create larger pieces such as articles, essays, or chapters and sections of books.

You can follow this writing structure with your mind map. Instead of thinking about what points to include, you think in terms of paragraphs and the sentences that will make up that paragraph. This method works great when you are given writing assignments with a page or word limit. You set the first level branches as the paragraph you will write with lower-level branches as the sentences that will make up that paragraph.

To demonstrate, let's pretend you are given a writing assignment to write a 500-word article. You know that 500 words come to about 1 to 1 ½ pages of text, so you estimate the assignment to require five to six well-developed paragraphs. With this estimate, you plan to write 1 introductory paragraph, 3-4 supporting paragraphs, and 1 concluding paragraph. Thus you will begin your mind map as follows:

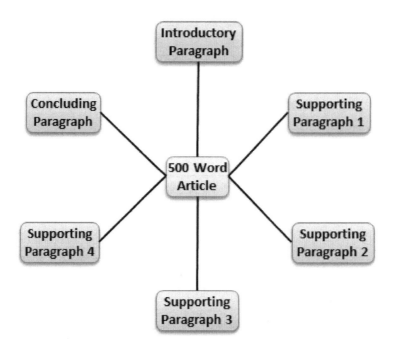

Then within each branch, you would add lower-level branches for the topic, supporting, and concluding sentences. The expanded image would look as follows:

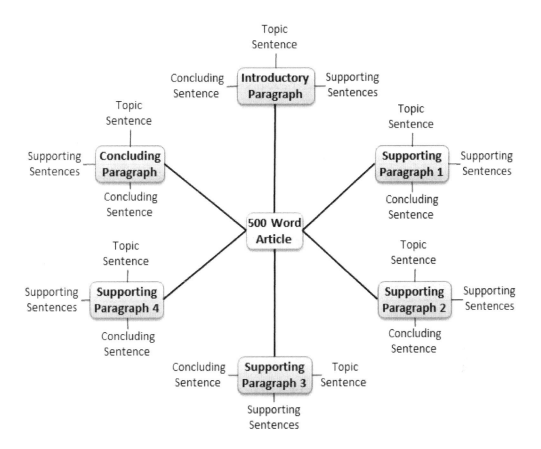

Now all you have to do is include in the lower-level branches what you want to say for each sentence. Once you do that, you will have everything neatly arranged to compose your piece. The only thing left to do is to take the sentences from each branch and assemble them into paragraphs for your article.

Writing Fiction

As touched on in the beginning of the chapter, fiction writing differs from non-fiction writing. Fiction does not follow the conventions of main topic, points, and supporting details nor does it follow the format of introductory sentence, body sentences, and concluding sentence. This style of writing focuses more on telling a story, and as a result, it is a more creative and imaginative endeavor.

One would think that because fiction writing is creative and imaginative, it would be more difficult to write. In some ways, that is true, but in many other ways, it is not. Even though fiction writing is creative and imaginative, it almost always follows a basic pattern. The pattern involves the use of literary elements such as character, plot, theme, setting, and conflict. Almost all fiction works—whether a fairytale, book, or movie—incorporate these elements. In the same way a non-fiction writer uses introductory, body, and concluding sentences to create factual pieces, a fiction writer uses these elements to create artistic, creative ones.

Let's examine these elements in detail, and more especially, how one can incorporate them into a mind map to ease the task of organizing and writing works of fiction.

Character—Characters are the participants in the story. They are the individuals the story is about. They can be real like people and animals, fictional representations of people and animals, or make-believe depictions of spirits, objects, even robots. The characters also define specific traits of the participants, such as physical appearance, personalities, attitudes, and behaviors.

The main classifications of characters include protagonist, antagonist, supporting, and minor. The protagonist is the main character. He or she is the hero or heroine in the story. The antagonist is the person who opposes the protagonist. This person is usually referred to as the villain. Supporting characters assist the main characters. Although the story does not evolve around them, they are essential to its unfolding. Minor characters are like extras in a movie or TV show. They play trivial roles and make short appearances.

Plot—Plot is the story line. It is the series of events that make up what the story is about. Plot is like the carrot on a stick that engages the readers of the story to make them want to keep reading.

There are 5 components to a plot—exposition, rising action, climax, falling action, and resolution. The exposition sets up the story. This is where the setting is established, characters are introduced, and the conflict is initiated. The rising action follows the exposition and through a series of complications, leads up to the climax. Climax is the single action-packed scene where the conflict of the novel is resolved. It is the moment of greatest danger for the characters, specially the protagonist. Falling action depicts the events after climax, showing the outcome of the climax and helping to bring the story to a close. Lastly, resolution is the conclusion, detailing how the story ends for all the characters.

Conflict—conflict is the struggle, predicament, or challenge the characters face. It is the fight, battle, opposition, barrier or hurdle that has to be overcome. This is the most important element, because a story without a conflict isn't really a story.

There are two types of conflict—internal and external. Internal conflicts address mental and emotional issues such as identity or overcoming one's fears and insecurities. External conflict deals with forces outside one's self. These forces can be anything from a monster to an overbearing father. External conflicts tend to fall into one of six categories—Man against Man, Man against Nature, Man against Society, Man against the Mystical/Paranormal, Man against Fate, and the most recent addition, Man against Technology.

Theme—Theme is the central message or meaning of the story. It is the lesson the writer wants the reader to take away. In many respects, the theme can be thought of as the moral of the story. It can also be a revelation about life or human behavior. Common themes in literature include *love is blind, you can't judge a book by its cover, believe in yourself*, etc.

Stories don't necessarily need to have a theme. Stories written solely for the purpose of entertainment, like comedies and Hollywood blockbusters, rarely have a theme. These works are purely a form of entertainment. On the other hand, some stories can have multiple themes. If a story does include a theme, it can be stated directly or implied by the actions and outcomes.

Setting—Setting is where a story takes place. It includes both time and location. Time includes the past, present, future, or a combination of the three. Location can be defined in the broad such as a city, state, and country or in the narrow like a room, house, and neighborhood. It can also be as general as in the northern suburbs or specific as in 18 E. Elm, Chicago, IL.

Setting goes beyond time and space. It incorporates characteristics such as weather and season as well. It also incorporates circumstances such as historical events and social/political issues. Used correctly, setting can help set the mood for the tale.

These are the literary elements of a story, and almost all fiction works employ them in one form or another. They are the essential ingredients for a good recipe. Since these elements are essential to all types of stories, you can use them as a basis for your mind map. You would commence with the title or general subject of the story. Then you would set the above elements as the first-level branches. It would look like this:

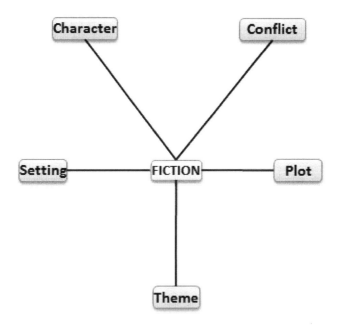

Moving forward, you would set the different aspects of each element as sub-branches. For example, around the main branch of *Plot*, you would put *exposition, rising action, climax, falling action*, and *resolution*. Within *Setting*, you would put time, location, and other related sub-branches. After we do this for the rest of the elements, our diagram will look as follows:

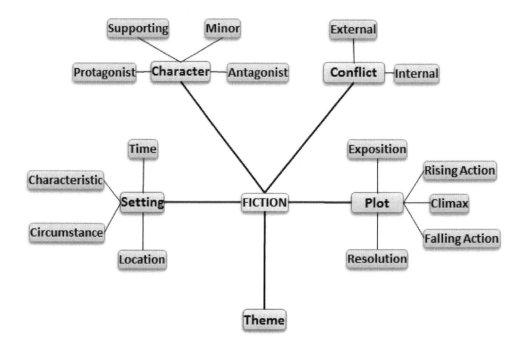

Now you have a starting point for your story. You have all the required elements laid out and have a big picture view of everything within those elements to address. At this point, you can start developing each one. You can look at *Plot* and branch out with ideas of how it will unfold from the exposition to the climax to the resolution. Then you can move to the next element like *Setting* to map out when and where the story will take place. Completing this for the remaining elements will sets the stage for youth tale. You can even move back and forth between the various elements to ensure that everything ties together. This gives you a nice platform to begin writing. You just have to put words to the elements you've prepared.

Fiction writing is not, of course, a high-priority task for most people. It is not a skill that average people need to be successful in their day-to-day lives, unless of course it is their profession. Although story telling may not be your profession, it may be a long-time goal of yours to write a play or novel. If you are a student, you may have to write a tale or two to get through a required course. Whatever your reason or motivation for writing fiction, you can use the above mind map as a template to guide you through the process. It can help you sketch out all the necessary elements to create a well-developed, thoroughly engaging tale.

This is one way to apply mind maps for fiction writing. You open with the title or potential title of a story, poem, or novel. Then you draw out branches for the literary elements and sub-branches for the individual aspects of those elements. From there you plow through to develop the engaging narrative.

Getting Specific

Another way to apply mind maps is to help you develop the specifics of any one of the story elements. That is, if you need to work out the description of a character or the special aspects of a conflict or setting, you can create a unique mind map that centers on that character or aspect.

Being specific is critical to a good story. An important part of storytelling is getting your readers to buy into it. You want to engage readers in such a way that they suspend their disbelief and temporarily accept your narrative to follow along with what you are presenting. This is achieved by having well-developed and thought-out characters and plot.

Think about books such as Lord of the Rings and Harry Potter or movies like Star Wars and Avatar. These books and movies are known for developing intricate character profiles, complex plotlines, and descriptive settings. It's for these reasons they have been widely successful. The specific details make fiction real to the reader. So the more specific you can be, the more likely you are to engage your reader.

For instance, when developing the protagonist, it helps to go beyond simply presenting him as the hero of the story. It helps to also talk about his appearance (what he looks like), give his background (where he comes from), discuss his personality (what are his likes and dislikes), and even bring up his relationships (who are his friends and family). You can also mention the needs and desires of this character. The 20th century American writer Kurt Vonnegut, famous for such stories as Cat's Cradle and Slaughterhouse-Five, says *every character should want something, even if it's only a glass of water.*

This applies to the other elements, like setting. You'll want to go past merely saying the story takes place twenty years ago in Los Angeles. You might mention the season, the weather, the temperature—is it clear skies or rainy and muggy? Incorporate the five senses. Describe what the city looks, smells, tastes, feels, and sounds like. Depending on the type of story, it may also help to talk about the social and political overtones of the period.

Again, you can use mind maps for this purpose. You can take an element or an individual aspect of an element and work out all of its underlining features. With the technique, you can whip up realistic character profiles, descriptive scenery, and captivating plotlines. To illustrate, we'll look at developing a character.

Let's say you are writing a short story about Ethan Devin, a veteran coming back from the Afghan war. You begin by putting his name in the center. Then you add branches about the specific characteristics you want to describe. You might start off with something like this:

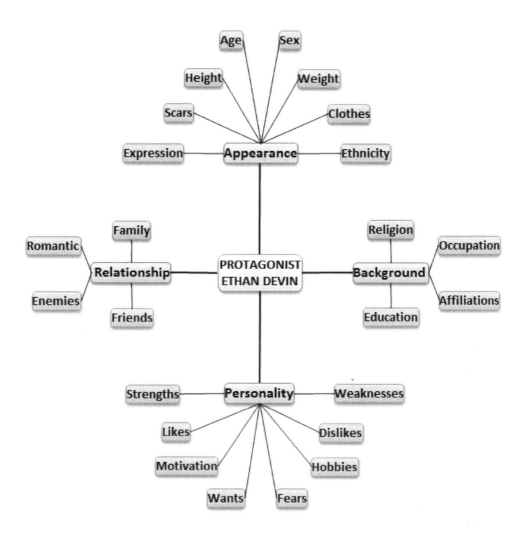

Looking at this mind map, you can see we broke up the character description into four categories—Appearance, Background, Personality, and Relationship. Within each category, we branched out specific aspects of the category we want to define. From here, we can work through each item to develop this character. We can detail his height and build, his family and friends, where he comes from, and more importantly, what makes him tick. All of this gives us a more realistic personality to engage our readers. Even though you may not mention every one of these descriptions in the story, your reader at an unconscious level will still pick up on the intricacies based on the actions and reactions this profile describes. You can use the above mind map as a template to develop all of your characters.

These are two ways you can go about using mind maps to help you write fiction. The first way uses a top-down approach. You start with a big picture view of all the important elements and work your way down developing each one. The second approach develops from the bottom up. Here you start with specific aspects of an element, and work your way up to the overall story.

You can use either method to outline all types of fictions—everything from novels, short stories, fables, and fairy tales to plays, films, comic books, and video games. The best thing about using mind maps for fiction writing (or nonfiction for that matter) is that because of the nonlinear format, you don't have to devote significant time to areas that are not ready and waste all of that motivation. Come back to it when you're ready. In the meantime, start developing other points as they come to you.

Mind maps are an excellent place to begin your planning as well. We discuss this in the next chapter.

CHAPTER 8 - PLANNING

Planning is the process of thinking about the activities required to achieve a desired result. It establishes a blue print or road map that tells you what you are going to do, when, and how. Many activities and events require planning such as a family vacation, wedding, business, or even marketing strategy.

Planning is critical for success. Those who spend time to plan tend to be more successful and achieve that success more quickly. That is because planning helps define a strategy while helping to avoid costly and time consuming mistakes. As the saying goes, if you fail to plan, you plan to fail.

Mind mapping is the ideal tool for planning. There are many reasons for this, but none more evident than their ability to help you simultaneously see your project in the big picture and smaller parts. In the big picture, you are able to view an entire project in one glance. Since each aspect of a project is defined by interconnecting branches, you can quickly see how all the individual branches come together to make the whole. In the smaller parts, you are able to dive into lower and lower levels to examine the intricacies involved. This way, you can follow a branch down to the individual parts to evaluate their effectiveness in ensuring the larger objectives can be met. This is the real benefit of creating plans with mind maps.

There are many ways to apply mind maps in this area. In fact, the possibilities are endless. Their application really depends on what you are trying to achieve. Putting together a vacation is different from putting together a business. Each pursuit has aspects to its success that are unique, thus requiring unique ways to assemble it into a mind map.

Although there are many ways to apply mind maps for planning, some strategies are quite universal. These strategies can be used to put together a wide variety of plans. One strategy is to use the questionary pronouns *who*, *what*, *where*, *when*, *why*, and *how*. Another is to divide large objectives into smaller components. Yet another involves thinking about timeframes. We will discuss all three below, starting with questionary pronouns.

Questionary Pronouns

As mentioned, questionary pronouns deal with answering the questions *who*, *what*, *where*, *when*, *why*, and *how*. This strategy is used heavily in journalism. When journalists report incidents on the news, they do so by providing answers to these questions. Delivering information within this framework helps viewers better understand what transpired. In the context of creating a plan, this framework helps you better identify all the items that need attention.

As always, start with the main topic. In this case, the main topic will be what you are planning. If it is a family vacation, put that in the center. If it is a wedding, that will be the main topic. When establishing the main topic, be as specific as possible. Instead of saying *Wedding*, you can say *John and Kathy's Wedding*.

From the center, draw out branches for each pronoun. Since there are six of them, you will draw six branches around the center. It will look as follows:

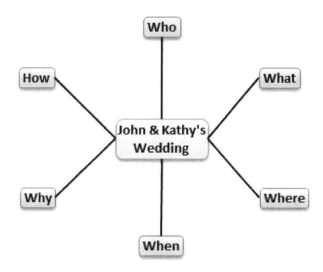

From here, go through and work out all the fine points of each pronoun. Below we discuss what you can or should include within each one.

Who—This identifies all the players. The players include individuals who will work on or are essential to making the plan happen. For example, if you are publishing a book, the essential individuals may include the writer, editor, proofreader, publisher, and distributor.

The players also include anyone who may be a recipient of the plan. That can include clients, customers, attendees, invitees, or an audience. In the example of book publishing, the recipients would be the readers or target audience of the book. Explore both in your analysis.

What—This outlines the items that need to be addressed to achieve the plan. It encompasses the many decisions, problems, choices, and challenges that you have to make, solve, pick, and overcome. In a marketing strategy for example, the *what* can include things such as the product, pricing, policy, packaging and everything in between.

Where—This defines the location. If it is an event, where will it be located? If it is a vacation, where will you be going? If it is a meeting, where will it be held? Depending on the nature of the event, you may have multiple locations to consider. In a wedding, for instance, you will have to consider locations not just for the ceremony, but for the reception and scenic photos as well.

When—The question here establishes the day and time the project is due or needs to be delivered. When evaluating this question, consider not only the plan as a whole, but the individual milestones as well. Take into account the intermediary deadlines necessary to keep the plan on time.

Why—The *why* is your reason for investing time, money, and resources in the project. It answers what you hope to accomplish and the end result you seek. It also establishes the fundamental benefits and root motivations that are driving the plan's existence. By addressing this in the beginning, you will have a better direction of how to proceed.

For certain types of plans, you will want to answer the *why* also with respect to your recipient. In a business plan for example, you will want to evaluate *why* customers will purchase your product. For a trade show, you will need to develop reasons *why* people will want to attend or sponsor your event. Understanding your customer's perspective will help you put together a more successful blueprint.

How—Here you establish ways to accomplish the plan. You will analyze the different options or avenues you have available. You can also evaluate your budget and financing. Other things to consider include how to manage risk, prioritize, and define success. Addressing these items manages the *how*.

Let's illustrate this by continuing with wedding planning as an example.

In a wedding, the *who* would include the organizers and the attendees. The organizers would likely include the wedding planner, DJ, caterers, ushers, photographer, even the priest. The attendees can be broken down into two groups: wedding party and guests. The guests can include your friends, family, co-workers, and acquaintances. These can be broken down further by guests of the groom and guests of the bride. The wedding party would include the best man, maid of honor, groomsman, bridesmaids, flower girl, and ring bearer. This branch would look as follows:

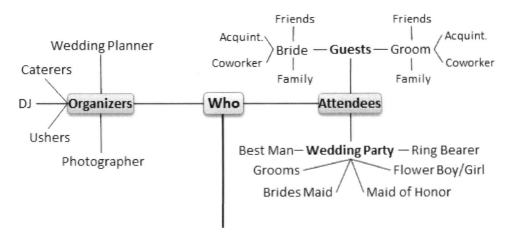

As it relates to *what*, the major decisions in a wedding involve the dress, cake, entertainment, flowers, and theme. Other decisions include the food menu, invitations, transportation, and guestbook. Some items will need to be divided further. For instance, with flowers, you will want to consider the bouquet, corsage, center piece, and boutonnieres. This branch would be set up as follows:

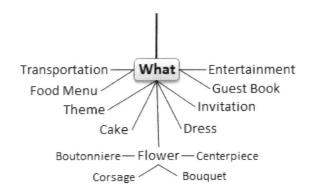

The next question deals with *where*. As mentioned before, you will have to address at least three *where* questions. Where would you like to hold the reception, where you would like to have the ceremony, and where would you like to take the scenic photos? You may want to throw in another one, where to have the rehearsal dinner? Within each sub-branch, you can list the possible choices. As you evaluate each choice, you can cross it off until you determine the best option. This is how to proceed with this branch:

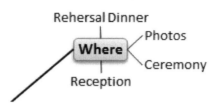

Next in line is *when*. The main *when* consideration is the wedding date. Other *when* considerations may include dates for sending out the invitation, the date when guests should RSVP, as well as dates for when deposits are due. You may have other dates related to specific *what* items. You can include them either as lower-level topics under the *what* branch or here.

Now let's discuss *why*. Why are you putting the plan together? For certain plans, like a wedding, the *why* is fairly obvious. You are planning the wedding to get married. However, it helps to take the answer one step beyond the obvious. That could be something like *To create a memorable evening that shares with friends and family the joy and excitement of two people coming together.* This kind of *why* will help guide you to create a better experience.

Lastly, the *how*. Here you will think about how you will finance the wedding, how you will work out the wedding dates, how will you find a planner, caterer, DJ, etc.

Putting it all together, you will have a mind map that looks like this.

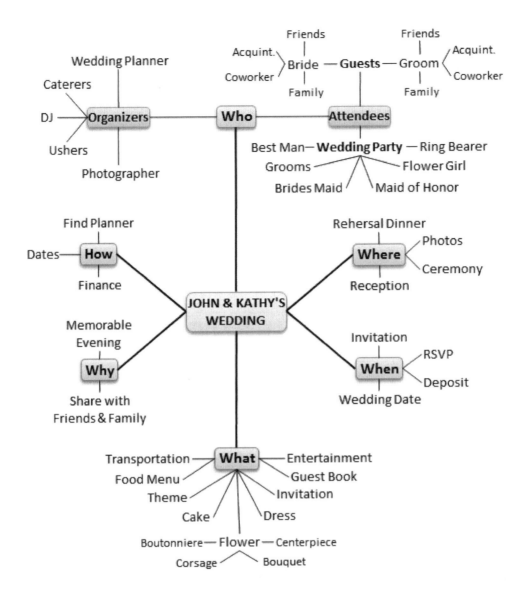

With this map, you have laid out the ground work for your plan. Now you can go through each branch and sub-branch to work out the details of who to invite, what cake to order, and the theme to use. You can cross out items that have been addressed, add branches to items that have additional dimensions or options, and so on.

This strategy is effective not just for planning, but also for writing, brainstorming, researching, investigating, storytelling, and reporting. You start with the basic questions of who, what, where, when, why and how around a topic or issue, and then you work through the essential details.

Components

The process we described above is one strategy for creating a plan. Another strategy is to look at the individual components. This requires breaking the plan down into its functional parts. From there, you work out the details of each part.

How you breakdown the parts will depend on the type of plan you are putting together. As mentioned, different plans have different considerations essential for their success. A business plan will require you to think about finances—what things are going to cost and where you are going to get money. Although a family vacation may require some financial planning, it will need more emphasis on what to do and where to go. On the other hand, a marketing proposal will focus primarily on a product, service, or information and how to get that product, service, or information into the hands of the consumer. The individual aspects of these plans would be the functional components you want to detail.

Let's continue with wedding planning to illustrate. We start by thinking about the major components of a wedding, such as entertainment, catering, photos, guests, attire, and the wedding party. These are the traditional components addressed in a typical western-style wedding; therefore we start with a mind map that looks as follows:

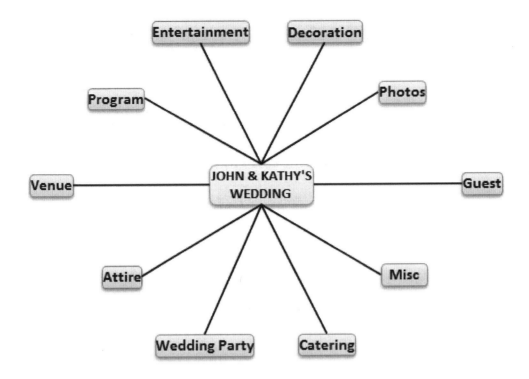

From here we go through the branches and plan out each component. For starters, we think about all of the things we need to consider for the entertainment. The main considerations include deciding on the songs to play, whether to have a DJ or band, and what diversions to offer kids. We list these items as sub-branches under entertainment. Then we move to another branch like catering. For catering we need to decide on a wedding cake, hors d'oeuvres, appetizers, dinner and dessert. We place these on the map as well.

You will follow this process for all of the branches. As you do this, let the ideas flow. Keep the primary ideas connected to the central idea, and then within lower-level topics let additional specific thoughts radiate outward. Don't overthink—pour everything out. After working through all the branches, you will have a mind map that looking like this:

Now you have your wedding all laid out. You have the major components placed in the first level branches, with critical details and decisions in the lower-levels. From here, you can go further and add even deeper branches. In them you can list options, pros and cons to the options, head count, and even the budget or the maximum amount you are willing to spend on the item. For example, under *guest*, you can estimate how many guests you can invite. Under *wedding party*, you can list possible choices for who you would like to have as the best man and maid of honor. For other items like *DJ*, *catering*, and *wedding dress*, you can list how much you are willing to spend to stay within budget as well as choices for possible suppliers.

If you notice, many of the items in this mind map are the same or similar to the one in the questionary pronoun example. The variation lies in that they are arranged differently. This is the versatility of mind maps. The structure allows you to deal with the same critical issues using multiple approaches.

Now, if you really want to be thorough in your planning, you can use both strategies. You can start with the interrogative pronoun strategy as a way to brainstorm and get all the essential considerations out on paper. Then you can move to this strategy and go more in depth. By doing both, you will be able to analyze and develop a more comprehensive plan.

Timeline

Thus far you have learned two ways to plan with mind maps. One uses questionary pronouns. The other breaks it down by functional components. Yet another strategy involves setting it up into a timeline. This type of plan requires thinking about activities in terms of when they need to be done or completed.

All plans have a deadline or due date. If they do not have a firm deadline, then they will likely have some sort of date range for completion. Since plans have deadlines, that means all the tasks and activities that make up a plan will also have deadlines. Given the target-oriented nature of plans, it can be handy to set up each task, chore, duty, function based on when it is due or needs to be completed.

In this way, you would organize what you need to do or have done at various junctures. For instance, if you had to direct a major project due ten months from now, you would decide what to have completed by month three, month six, month nine, as well as one month, week, and day before the deadline. A plan like this lays out tasks in chronological order.

To mind map a plan this way, you start by determining the length of the project. From there, you divide the timeframe into milestones. The milestone can be daily, weekly, monthly, quarterly, or as in the above example, a combination. Each milestone would be represented by a branch on the map. Within each branch, you would plan out or think through what you would like to do or have done in that milestone.

Let's review the wedding example one more time. You and your partner have decided to come together in matrimony. You want the wedding to be in the summer, so you set July 16 as the date. It's fall now, so that gives you exactly 9 months to the big day. With 9 months, you decide to break down your timeline by scheduling what to accomplish in the first three months, by month six, the two months after that, and one month, two weeks, one week, and day before, as well as the day of the wedding. The first level branch would be set up like so:

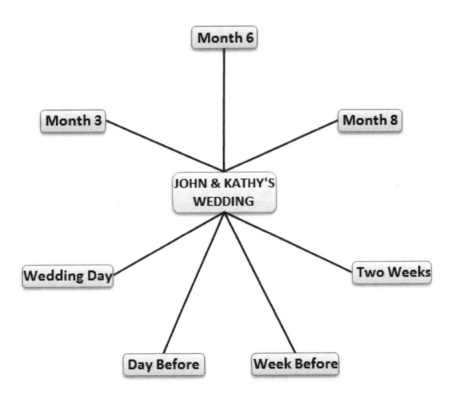

Then for each branch, you determine what to do or have completed by that date. By the first three months, you may want to announce the wedding, select the wedding date, hire a consultant/coordinator, determine the theme, and decide on a head count. By month six, you may want to book the caterer, select the photographer, put together the guest list, and pick out the florist, venue, and wedding party. For the next two months, you will want to send out the invitations, try on wedding dresses, and select entertainment. Once you complete this for all the milestones, your mind map will have a look similar to this:

At this stage, you have a complete schedule outlined for your wedding. You have noted everything you need to do or have completed for each milestone down to the big day. This is yet another effective strategy.

Earlier we noted that you can combine the questionary pronoun strategy with the components strategy to help you develop a more comprehensive plan. If you wanted, you could incorporate this into the mix too. You could start with the first two strategies to uncover all aspects of your plan. From there you could put the plan into a timeline. This will ensure that you address all the critical issues and decisions in a timely manner.

CHAPTER 9 - LISTS

Another noteworthy function of mind maps is to create lists. By *lists*, we mean any collection or ordering of items. Although mind maps can be used to put together a diverse assortment of lists, the two most common include shopping and to-do lists. We will discuss these two varieties in detail below. This is not a complicated application of the technique, so you can take what you learn here and apply it to other types of lists.

SHOPPING LISTS

With traditional shopping lists, you simply create a long inventory of the items that you want to remember to buy. With mind maps, however, you can be creative. With this method, you can put together lists that are more carefully considered and organized. Below is an example that illustrates this.

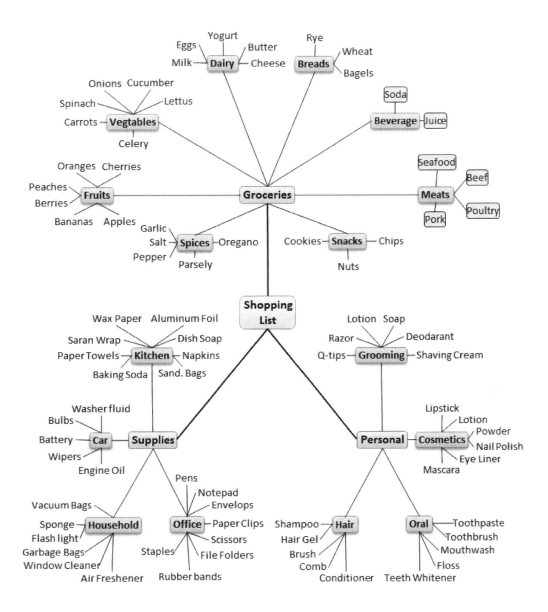

As you can see above, we noted each item by category. We put groceries on top, personal items on the bottom right, and supplies to the bottom left. Then within each branch, we added the individual items we wanted to remember to purchase.

Mind mapping in this way helps you easily think of all the items to remember. With linear note taking, you have to think about every item you need to buy, then write it down. With a mind map, you begin with categories. As you learned in the chapter on brainstorming, when you think of a word like groceries, your brain instantly connects that word to the items related to it. So all you need to do is take the items your mind associates with the category, and write down those ones you need to buy. This way, you are not trying to recall separately each and every article for your list.

The other benefit of mind mapping your shopping is efficiency. When you create a list like the one above, as mentioned, you do so in categories. At the store, items are usually shelved in similar categories. At a grocery store, for example, dairy items are all placed together, meats are all next to each other, and so on. Thus when you shop, you can go to the dairy section, grab everything on your map for that category, cross the category off your list, go to the meat section and grab everything in that category, and go on to the next category until your shopping is done.

On the other hand, if you went to the store searching for items one by one, you would be doing a lot of back and forth between the same isle and sections of the store, wasting a lot of time to ensure you have everything on your sheet. The mind map way makes you more efficient.

To save even more time, one thing you can do with a shopping list is create a mind map template with only high level categories, like the one shown below.

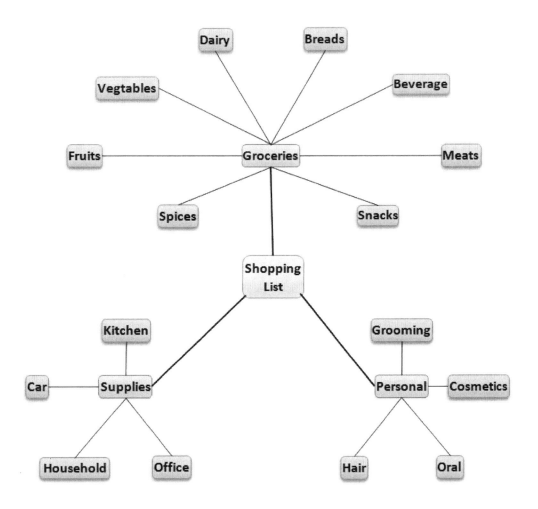

This template does not include the individual items to buy, only the groupings. If you keep several copies of the template in your kitchen drawer, each time you go shopping, you can take one of the copies, fill it out with the items you want to remember to buy, and then take it with you to the store. It is that easy.

An alternative way to group the above list of items is by location. If your shopping needs require you to visit several stores, you can create a mind map that arranges items within the store they are located. For example, I like to buy my personal, household, and kitchen supplies at the department store. I find that a department store has the lowest prices when it comes to these types of products. I don't buy food here as I buy organic, and so I shop at the local organic grocery store.

Unfortunately, the organic grocery store does not have a good selection of meats, so I go to Bob's Meat Market around the corner to purchase meats. For bread, I go to Martha's Bakery; for car supplies, I go to Lee's Auto, and for office supplies I go to Office Depot. Therefore, I put together a list like so:

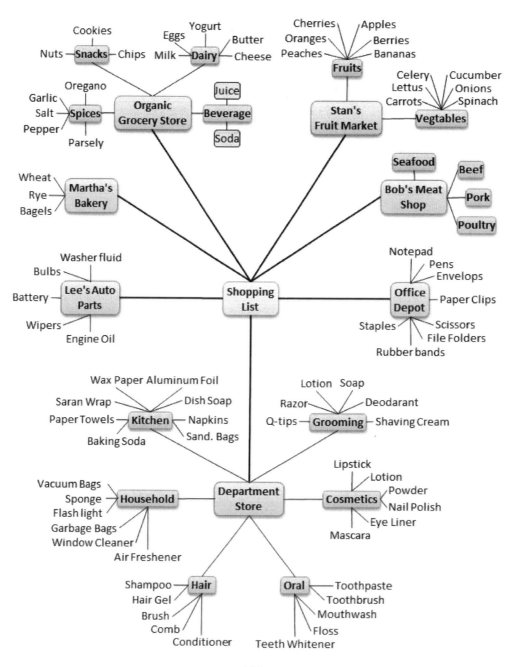

I first drive to the department store to get everything on the list. Then I drive to the grocery store to buy all my groceries. Then I'm off to the fruit market. Afterwards, I go to the meat shop and then to the next store and to the one after that. Before I know it, my list is complete and I can enjoy the rest of my weekend.

The above two examples show you the versatility of mind maps. They both contain the same items, but are organized two different ways. Which one you use is up to you.

In addition, you can tailor your mind map for specific situations or events. For example, if you are hosting a Super Bowl party or catering a family gathering, you can create a mind map that addresses all the items you will need for that function. In the center you will put the name of the event. Around the center you will put the categories. Then within each category, you will put the items you want to remember to buy.

TO-DO LISTS

Shopping lists are not the only type of list for which mind maps are effective. Mind Maps are a great way to organize your tasks into a handy to-do list. As with a shopping list, the traditional way to put together a to-do list is to write a line-by-line inventory of all the things you want to accomplish. With mind maps, you can be more systematic. Also, you can organize tasks in many ways, allowing you to develop to-do lists that help you be more resourceful and productive.

Perhaps, for example, you have a lot on your plate this week. The dishes need cleaning, the lawn needs mowing, and you need gas, an oil change, and a wash for your car. In addition, you have assignments for school to complete. To add to your already busy schedule, you also need to clean the house, go to the bank, and call your mom. All this can be quite overwhelming to think about, let alone remember.

With a mind map, it is easy to organize everything. You get under way by figuring out how you want to group all of the tasks. Each group will represent a distinct branch for your mind map. A simple standard is to organize items under *personal*, *home*, *car*, and depending on whether you are a student or employee, *school* or *work*. Then within each branch, you list the tasks you need to complete. Below is an example of how this would look.

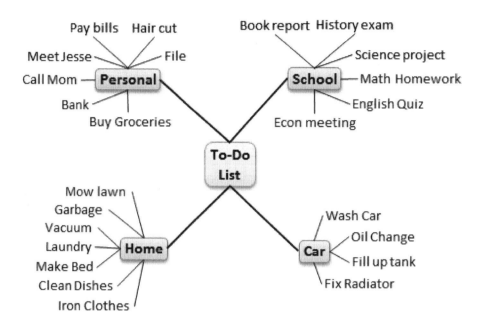

If you notice, you have all of your tasks written down so you will remember them. Also, they are laid out spatially and grouped together making them neatly organized. More importantly, they are arranged in a way that allows you to see clearly which areas need more time and attention. This is one way to arrange a list of to-do items.

Another way to arrange your to-do items is by the days of the week. Take a look at this example:

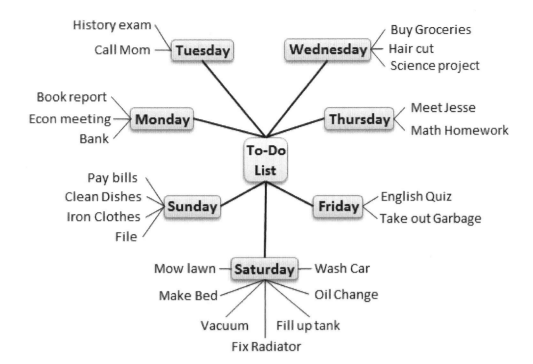

The above sample has the same set of tasks, but they are organized by the days of the week. In this way, you list tasks on days you plan to do them and/or on the days they are due. This too effectively organizes your work week.

You can use mind maps in this way to plan out a whole month. To do so, set the first level branches as the weeks of the month. Set the second level branches as the days of the week. Here is an illustration:

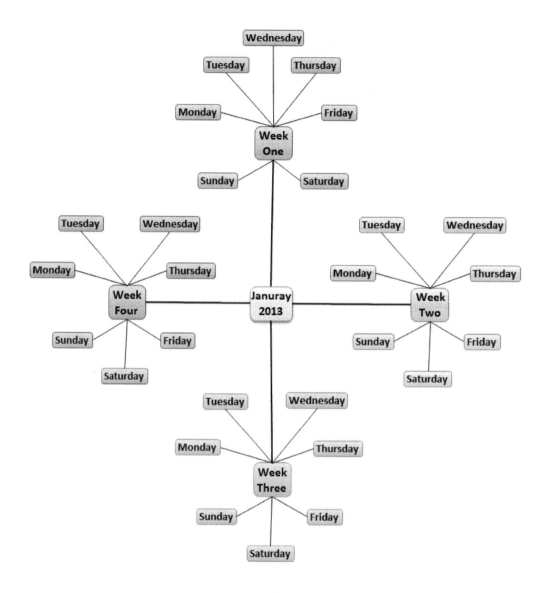

From here, list what you will do or need to have done on or by that day. This is helpful because you have a big picture of your schedule. You don't have to flip through the many pages of a calendar to see when you are busy and when you are free because the information is easy to see in one glance.

Often a task requires you to do several things in order for it to be considered complete. In these instances, you can break down larger tasks into smaller parts and list those parts as sub-branches within a task. For example, the task of fixing the radiator requires taking your car to mechanics, getting quotes, scheduling a time for the repair, and finally, hiring the person to the do the job. In your mind map, under *Fix radiator*, you can create sub-branches that list these as sub-steps. As you complete each sub-step, you can cross it off your list until the task is fully complete. You can create as many sub-steps and go as deeply into lower and lower levels as you feel necessary to complete the task.

As with a shopping list, the benefit of mind mapping your to-do list is that it helps you more easily recall items you need to remember. By thinking of high level responsibilities in your life, it is easy to think of lower-level tasks that need to be done. Otherwise you are struggling to remember each individual task and worrying if you forgot to add something.

Another benefit is that a list like this is more encouraging to look at than a long and lengthy inventory of to-do items. Looking at such items can be overwhelming and can create feelings of apprehension. This can discourage you from starting. You may not know where to begin nor how. It makes accomplishing the list feel like a chore.

When your list is separated in the form of a mind map, however, it is more inviting and creates less apprehension. You know exactly what areas need work, and more specifically, what tasks within each area. Things are not jumbled together, so you don't feel overwhelmed. You are more motivated to start and finish everything.

As with a shopping list, you can create a template for your to-do list. You can create a mind map outline of high-level responsibilities you work on regularly. Each time you need to write out a list, you can pull out a copy of the template, fill it with errands and tasks, and then you're on your way.

Like a shopping list, you can also vary your mind map for specific situations and create a to-do list to address items you need to accomplish for specific events like moving, planning, and traveling.

This is all as it relates to lists. As indicated earlier, this is not a complicated application of mind maps. You can easily transfer the instruction here to other directory or catalogue type information. Next on the agenda is goal setting.

CHAPTER 10 - GOAL SETTING

Goal setting is the process of outlining an objective or ambition that you want to accomplish. It is an achievement tool used by students, athletes, and professionals to help them excel. Examples of popular goals include losing weight, getting a promotion, or quitting a habit.

The concept of goal setting has been around for ages. If you have heard anything about it, you know its good practice to set and write goals. Our purpose here is not to validate the technique, but to introduce mind mapping as an enhanced method for setting goals.

A goal-setting mind map is something of a cross between a plan and a to-do list. When setting a goal, people usually have a general idea of the outcome. Though they still need to work out exactly what it is they want to do, similar to the way that a planning mind map can be used to organize a plan. Once the person knows the specifics of their goal, he or she can then determine milestones, action items, and deadlines. This part of the goal- setting mind map is much like a to-do list.

Let's look more closely at how to set goals with mind maps. Since mind mapping for goals is similar to mind mapping plans and to-do lists, this chapter will not be quite as long as those chapters. If you have read them, you will have a strong understanding of the core features, so there is no need to repeat the same information. Nonetheless, we will still provide explanations, instructions, and an example specific to goals.

First, start with what you would like to achieve as the main topic. If you are taking the time to sit down to make a goal-setting mind map, you probably already have a general idea of what you wish to accomplish. Maybe you would like to lose weight, learn C++, open a restaurant, get straight A's in school, or grow a garden. Whatever result you seek, that will be your main topic.

When you are defining the main topic, be as descriptive as possible. The more descriptive you can be, the more detail you will have for your goal. More detail makes it easier to plan and achieve your goal. Examples of descriptive goals might include *Lose 30 lbs.*, *Open a Family Restaurant*, or *Grow Shade-Loving Plants*.

Next, break the goal down with subtopics. Every goal can be broken down into smaller, functional parts. The best way to split your goal is to do what makes the most sense to you. A goal of losing weight could have subtopics of diet, exercise and lifestyle, or it could be separated by time periods—month 1, month 2, etc. Perhaps someone else who is making a goal of losing weight would divide their goal by progress markers—2 inches off waist, 1 inch off thigh, etc. It's all about how you look at your goal and what divisions make sense to you.

Once you have established your subtopics, the next step entails listing lower-level topics. With a goal-setting mind map, you will find that you have several options in deciding what to include in the lower-levels. Some lower-level topics can be milestones while others can list ideas and steps to help reach your goal. In all there are three things you should focus on with this step.

Milestones—Milestones set smaller goals on the way to the main goal. They create a kind of check list of how much you have done and how far you have to go. They often mark important points in reaching your goal. Examples of milestones might be *lose 5 lbs.*, *obtain business license* or *assemble a garden*. Some goals will have more milestones than others. Starting a business will include a large number of milestones, each something you have to do before you can open the doors. Losing weight will usually have a smaller number of milestones to mark your progress.

Action Items—Action items list the tasks and activities required to achieve the set target or milestone. They are the *how* of meeting your goals. Examples of action items include *run 15 minutes a day, ask Small Business Administration rep about things I don't know,* and *buy garden hose and sprinkler.* Like milestones, some goals will have many action items while others will not. Losing weight is a goal that will have a number of tasks involving diet, exercise, lifestyle changes, and anything else required to lose weight. Opening a business will have even more tasks.

Deadlines—Deadlines in a goal-setting mind map are just like deadlines anywhere else. They tell you how long you have to get something done. If your goal doesn't come with a built-in deadline (raise $X before going to college, for instance), then you may want to create one. Losing 30 lbs. is a goal that doesn't have any specific time limit, but it can help you stay motivated if you assign yourself a deadline—say by the holidays, before summer, or even better, May 30th 2015.

You can assign a deadline for each milestone and action time. Someone whose aim is to attend college has the deadline to take standardized exams, the deadline to submit early applications, and the deadline to submit regular applications. Other examples of deadlines include *open by holiday season next year* and *finish planting by June 1.*

Once you have piled on the lower-level topics, your goal-setting mind map is finished. The complete mind map will present a detailed description of your goal and a general plan for achieving it. Use this map to work towards your goal by following the milestones and action items you established.

Let's take a look at Sandy, who is working on a goal to start a new business. She has already spent some time brainstorming and knows that she wants to open a restaurant in her home town. Sandy starts her mind map by putting *Open Restaurant* as the main topic.

Next, Sandy considers subtopics. She could have subtopics such as *Need to Have/Want to Have*. She might divide her goal by stages of work, for instance *Research/Preparation/Action*. Eventually, she decides to use two subtopics, *Business* for activities related to the business side of owning a restaurant and *Restaurant* for activities related to running a restaurant.

Now it is time to really flesh out her goal. Under the subtopic of *Restaurant*, Sandy puts descriptions like *home cooking*, *cozy*, *good food*, and *informal*. Each of these lower-level branches help to specify her goal–the kind of restaurant she wants to open. Branches under the *Business* subtopic become a mix of goal descriptions *open in 1 year*, *generate $x Profit*, etc., and things she needs to do to achieve her goal—*write business plan*, *apply for loan*, and *find location*.

When Sandy is done, she has a detailed mind map describing exactly what it is she wants to do and many of the steps she needs to take in order to do it. You can use the same process to create a mind map for your own goals. Start with the general aim or objective as the main topic. Then decide how to break the objective down into parts. Add detail for each part of your goal with a mix of descriptions of what you want and ideas for how to get it. When you are done, you'll have a mind map that can help you achieve any ambition.

CHAPTER 11 - THEMATIC PROJECTS

Creative projects cover a wide range of activities from building a house to writing a novel to making a movie. Mind maps can be used with creative projects in ways that have been described in the earlier chapters. For instance, a group that is making a movie can use to-do list or goal-setting mind maps to schedule their tasks. Although these types of tasks can be scheduled with outlines or traditional organization tools, as you have learned, the mind map way can work better and be more efficient.

There is another type of creative work called thematic projects. Thematic projects are creative endeavors that focus on conveying a theme or idea, rather than a linear story (like a novel) or a concrete object (like a house). Love, sorrow, family, nature, and other themes permeate song, sculpture, painting, and poetry. It is important to point out that when we say *thematic*, the reference is similar to *theme* as it relates to the literary elements of fiction writing discussed in chapter 7. In that context, theme meant *message* or *lesson*, in a sense, that is what thematic projects convey.

Traditional and linear tools are even less effective with thematic projects because they are difficult to clearly define and they don't respond well to attempts to being put in a box. It is difficult for a songwriter to use an outline to plan a song or for an oil painter to reduce his work to a to-do list. The final product of these projects conveys ideas that these tools can't readily grasp.

Unlike other tools, mind maps can help people working on thematic projects. They can help artists organize and prepare their thoughts and ideas before beginning their work. Thematic projects use associations to convey the theme the artist is working on. Since mind maps promote associative organization, they can help artists establish how to best convey their theme.

Consider Daniel, a song writer. Daniel wants to write a song about a father's love. That will be the main topic of his mind map—*a father's love*. He writes that in the middle of his paper and thinks about what this theme means to him and how he can write a song about it.

Daniel decides that there are two main paths for his theme—the imagery of his lyrics and the mood of his music—so he makes two subtopics: *Imagery* and *Mood*. Now he is ready for the details that will shape his song. Under *Mood* he puts lower-level topics that describe how the music should sound. Some of them include *quiet*, *strong*, *major chord*, and *supportive base line*. In Daniel's mind, music with these qualities describes a father's love.

Imagery then has lower-level topics that describe moments and images that Daniel associates with a father's love. He might add branches for *holding son for the first time*, *learning to drive*, and *summer days fishing*. When Daniel is done, he has a mind map for imagery, ideas, and descriptors that he will combine to make his song. This is one path to developing a thematic project.

Sometimes a thematic project develops in a different fashion. Theresa is a painter who works in watercolors. One day she gets an idea for a painting of hidden spring in a forest. She does a quick sketch so she doesn't lose the image. When she translates the sketch into a painting, she wants it to be powerful and moving. She knows there is a meaning to this image, but isn't sure what it is or how to make it fully *real* in her painting. Thus she starts a mind map.

The main topic for Theresa's mind map will be *Hidden Spring in a Forest*. As a painter, Theresa is a visual person, and rather than writing out *Hidden Spring in a Forest*, she uses the sketch she made as the main topic. Now she can let ideas and images related to the hidden spring become part of her diagram. First she decides that the spring being hidden is important, so that becomes one of her subtopics. Next, the forest is important, so she makes that another subtopic. Lastly, she wants the final painting to really play with light and shadow, accordingly that becomes yet another subtopic.

Theresa continues thinking about her idea and the subtopics on her mind map. To her, *hidden* relates to *secret*, so she writes that down as a lower-level topic. *Secret* has associations for Theresa with *sacred*. She writes that down as well and puts a star next to it—she's found one of her themes. In the meantime, Theresa sees the forest as being dark and ominous. She writes down *menacing* as a lower-level topic within forest. This gives her the idea of a crow or raven in the forest spying on the spring. She writes that image down as something to add to her painting to help convey her theme. Thinking about light and shadow, it's now obvious to her that the spring should be bright, with a shaft of sunlight almost making it glow; while the forest should be dark and full of shadows.

Theresa continues developing each sub and lower-level topic. Over time, she fills in her mind map with themes, ideas, and smaller details to add to her painting. This gives her a better starting point. She will no longer be painting randomly, hoping that something unique comes out. With mind maps, she can more precisely expand her vision. This is an alternative to developing a thematic project.

Using a mind map to plan thematic assignments is actually a combination of planning and brainstorming. The associative nature of a mind map helps you think of things that relate to your theme. At the same time, you can plan how to include these themes into the project. The ability to simultaneously brainstorm and plan makes mind mapping a useful tool for these types of tasks. Let's break it down step by step.

First, begin with the idea that you want to turn into a thematic project. Maybe the idea is a sculpture you want to design or a few lines of lyrics you want to turn into a great song. Whatever the idea, set it as the main topic. When you set it, you can do it in whichever way makes the most sense to you. You can write out chords, sketch an image, or even scribble a haiku. Use the option that works best for your thought process.

Then, take a few minutes to think about the project and come up with some subordinate concepts related to your main topic. These could be images, phrases, or anything else that jumps out as central to the project. A good way to do this is to ask yourself *what are the most important parts of this project*? Write these subordinate insights down as subtopics.

Next, think about what you associate with these subtopics. What images come to mind? What chords or motifs? The things that you associate with your key ideas, the things that jump into your mind when you think about your key ideas, become the lower-level topics for your mind map. Like your main topic, these lower-level topics can be words, sketches, key signatures, or any other notations that work to record the thought.

When you are done with your mind map, it should include all the critical factors from central images and lyric phrases to tempo and mood. The mind mapping process lets you pull together all your thoughts and ideas about your project. This way you know everything to include in order to finish your work.

In the next chapter we're going to take a look at how to apply mind maps in a group setting.

CHAPTER 12 - GROUP MIND MAPPING

Mind maps are tools not just for individuals, but for groups as well. Groups of people working together can tackle larger and more difficult projects than one person alone. A group using a mind map can break down even the most complicated project into manageable steps and use that map to coordinate themselves and their tasks.

Groups can get the most out of a mind map when they make it together. While one person can make a mind map for a group to work from, it is better for it to be made by everyone working collectively. One benefit of mapping this way is that it puts everyone *on the same page* in terms of the project and its goals. Additionally, more people working leads to more ideas and better solutions to problems.

Group mind mapping has some unique challenges. A mind map illustrates connections between ideas, but every person understands things differently. A group mind map has to have connections that are understood by everyone in the group. Another problem that arises is that more people working on a map means more disagreements about what to include as main, sub, and lower-level topics. Nevertheless, if everyone in the group can come together and be willing to make compromises, these difficulties can be managed.

There are a number of ways a group can create a mind map. It really depends on the dynamic of the group. Below are three strategies with which you can experiment. Select the method that best fits your group's dynamic.

Project Lead Mind Mapping

Project lead mind mapping hinges on a person leading the group to coordinate the mind map. This type of group mind mapping works for groups that have a recognized leader. Business projects under the direction of a manager can do well with this method. Students working together on a school project or other groups that don't have someone in charge would do better with a different method. To mind map with a project lead, follow these steps:

Step 1—The project lead chooses the main idea of the mind map. Often the main idea will be easy to identify. For instance, if the group is going to be developing and marketing a new product for a company, then the main idea could be as simple as *new product*. If the group is in charge of planning a holiday party, then the main idea would be *holiday party*.

Let's pretend that a group from a small business is working on a plan for a new product in development. The project lead uses the name of the new product as the main topic of the mind map. She starts the mind map by writing the product name in the center of a white board.

Step 2—After picking the main topic, the project lead sits down with the group to determine subtopics for the mind map. Members of the group make suggestions for possible subtopics and discuss each suggestion. The project lead may offer her own suggestions, ask opinions of group members who are shy or not active in the discussion, and take other actions to get the best possible ideas from the group. The project lead will pick what she thinks are the best suggestions for subtopics and notes them down.

In our example, the project lead gets the discussion started and sits back to listen to the group's ideas. After a few minutes of brainstorming, she picks three subtopics that describe the stages of new product development. She writes the new subtopics on her white board: *design*, *product testing* and *marketing*.

Step 3—After the project lead picks subtopics, the same process is repeated for the lower-level topics. The group makes suggestions and discusses the pros and cons of each suggestion. The project leader uses this discussion to help her determine which lower-level topics to add. If the project leader wants the mind map to be four layers deep, the process is repeated once again.

The project leader starts the discussion with design. The discussion leads to a number of suggestions for areas that the design team needs to do. The project lead eliminates some suggestions and picks four that she thinks are important: *dimensions*, *style*, *features* and *appearance*. The lead then moves on to the discussion of product testing. When the project lead is done adding all the lower-level topics she gathers from the group, she will have a working map with everyone's input.

Project lead mind mapping has several advantages. An active project lead can make certain that everyone's ideas are heard, even in a large group, ensuring that as many suggestions as possible are considered. At the same time, having one person in charge of deciding which suggestions make their way onto the map prevents arguments. Finally, with one person making the decisions, everything on the map will connect in a coherent fashion. The benefits of project lead mind mapping make it an ideal approach for groups with a recognized or appointed leader.

Consensus Mind Mapping

Consensus mind mapping is group mind mapping without a formal leader or manager. It is based on everyone in a group coming together and agreeing on each part of the mind map. This method of mind mapping works best with small groups or groups with members who are able to compromise and reach agreements easily. To group mind map with no established leader, follow these steps:

Step 1—The group sits down together and discusses possible main topics for their mind map. Each member of the group contributes his or her ideas and discusses their reasoning involved in choosing the main topic. Eventually the group comes to an agreement on the main topic.

Consider the same example as before—a group is drawing up a mind map as a plan for a new product. They sit down together with a white board or large piece of paper and discuss ideas for the main topic. After some conversation, they decide to use the name of the new product as their main topic. A member of the group writes this down in the center of the paper and the discussion begins on the subtopics.

Step 2—Members of the group make suggestions for subtopics. The group discusses each subtopic and agrees whether or not to add it to the mind map. If there is disagreement over a potential subtopic, the group works together to come up with a compromise or alternative that everyone can accept. When everyone comes to an agreement, the subtopics are added to the mind map.

In the example group, a number of suggestions are made for subtopics. Everyone agrees that *marketing* the new product should be a subtopic. One member suggests *design* and *product testing* as other subtopics. Someone else feels that design and product testing should be a lower-level topic under a different branch—product development. After some debate, the group agrees to use design and product testing as subtopics because they will involve different people.

Step 3—Lower-level topics are discussed in the same fashion as subtopics. The group discusses each one in turn. As they agree to lower-level branches for each subtopic, they move to the next. These branches are added to the mind map after agreement is reached.

The group discussing their new product starts out discussing the various things the design team will need to do. They agree on sub-branches for design and move on to discussing product testing. After some discussion, the group agrees that product testing will need to include both a *quality check* to make sure the new product works and a *consumer panel* to confirm that people will like it. When they finish discussing lower-level topics and branches for product testing, they write them down and begin the discussion of marketing.

This method of mind mapping offers advantages to groups who work well together. Consensus mind mapping takes advantage of the ideas and opinions of every member of the group, so the group has the best possible mind map. The final mind map is also a synthesis of the ideas, built around connections and concepts that everyone in the group agrees on and understands. Consensus mind mapping is not for every group creating a mind map, but it is a very good technique.

Individual Input Mind Mapping

Individual-input mind mapping is a more complicated method of group mind mapping, more complicated than either project lead or consensus strategies. It also has the disadvantage that the final result may be less coherent than mind maps made using other methods. However, it is an extremely thorough system of mind mapping that insures all possible ideas are included in the final diagram. This method works well for larger groups and groups that do not have a recognized leader. Here is how it works:

Step 1—The group first discusses and picks a main topic. This should be straightforward as the group ought to be aware why they are coming together to make a mind map in the first place. If there are minor disagreements over the main topic, the majority rules. If, on the other hand, there is extensive disagreement or debate, then there is clearly significant miscommunication as to the purpose of the group's work. When this happens, rather than beginning a mind map, the group should take the time to go back over their goals and intentions and make sure there is agreement about what the group is trying to accomplish. Consider using a group mind map to produce an idea for the main topic instead.

Going back one last time to the example of a small business releasing a new product, the group doesn't spend too much discussing the main topic. They are meeting to plan for the release of a new product, so they decide on the name of the new product as their main topic.

Step 2—Next, the group adds subtopics. To do this, each member of the group will suggest the subtopics they think should be a part of the mind map. When no one can think of any other subtopics to add, the group will discuss each suggested subtopic. If there is no general agreement on whether or not a subtopic should be added, the group will vote on it. The ones that are agreed on or voted in are added to the map.

The group working on a mind map for their new product generates 4 possible subtopics: *development, design, product testing,* and *marketing.* Everyone agrees with *marketing,* but the other three subtopics need to be put to a vote. *Development* is voted down, while *design* and *product testing* are chosen to be added.

Step 3—Adding lower-level topics is the longest part of this method, largely because most mind maps have far more lower-level branches than main branches. Going around the group, each person will contribute one lower-level branch to the mind map. They can contribute to any subtopic. After everyone in the group has had a chance to suggest one lower-level branch, go around the group again for a second round of suggestions. Continue going around the group adding sub-branches until no one has any further suggestions.

When no one can suggest anymore lower-level topics, give each person a chance to point out changes or modifications they think should be made. Good suggestions for changes include pointing out duplicate topics, offering reasons to move a topic from one branch to another, or correcting mistakes or contradictions within the diagram as a whole. Discuss each suggested change briefly. If there isn't agreement about a suggested change, put it to a vote. These suggestions allow the group to correct any problems in the map and to remove topics that lack consensus.

In the example, our group goes around the table each offering a lower-level suggestion. Next they each propose changes they think should be made. One person wants to remove the subheading *style* because he feels that the mind map doesn't need both *style* and *appearance*. After some discussion, the group votes on the suggestion. Most members of the group feel that style and appearance are different enough that both should be included in the map, so the suggestion to remove is dropped. When all suggestions have been discussed or put through a vote, the group then reads over the final mind map and votes to determine whether or not it is acceptable to the group.

Mind maps made with this method can be useful for large projects that require input from multiple people and departments. The method generates a great deal of opinions in the map. It also allows for a very thorough analysis and review to ensure everything is in good standing and everyone is on the same page. While this type of group mind mapping requires more time than most groups wish to spend, the effort leads to a very thorough analysis of the underlining project.

These are the three ways to mind map in a group. They are not the only way for a group to make mind maps. Other possibilities exist. For example, if everyone in the group is familiar with mind mapping, each member can make his or her own diagram that the group can bring together into one big map. Once you are comfortable with group mind mapping, you may come up with your own style or method that thrives with your personnel. Until then, use the ones described here as a starting place to get accustomed to mind mapping together.

This is all as it relates to other uses of mind maps. As you can see, mind maps are a very robust tool that can be used for a wide range of projects, activities, tasks, and problems. After reading this section, you may be able to come up with ideas of your own. If you do, put them to use. It may be just the thing you need to take your assignment or project to the next level. Now that we are finished here, let's move to the next section and learn other related methods.

SECTION IV

OTHER RELATED METHODS

Mind maps are not the only tool available for organizing ideas in a visual or associative fashion. Other tools exist such as flow charts, concept maps, and cognitive maps. These are mind mapping's close relatives. In this section, you will learn more about these relatives and the benefits they offer.

The question that naturally arises is *if mind maps are such a wonderful device for organizing ideas and learning, why would anyone need anything else?* The answer is as great as mind maps are, they more or less do one thing—explore a single idea to its fullest. Though, they do this one thing very well and are very adaptable.

Sometimes however, you need to do something other than explore a single idea. This is where other visual tools come in. If used properly, these tools can provide benefits in areas where mind maps fall short. Each one is special and serves a unique purpose. Since each serves a unique purpose, each can help with specific situations and problems.

Anytime you are looking to explore a single idea, pull out a mind map. For other tasks, try the other tools. Let's take a detailed look at these relatives, how they work and how they can help you.

CHAPTER 13 - FLOW CHARTS

A flow chart is a method for mapping processes. A process is the series of steps or actions that take you from a starting point to a desired outcome. For instance, if you wanted to make an ice cream cone, you would follow a process that involved selecting a cone, picking a flavor, and scooping the ice cream into the cone. Your starting point is *wanting an ice cream cone*, your outcome is *having an ice cream cone*, and the process is the steps in between.

A process can have multiple starting points as well as multiple outcomes. Think about the process a call center or customer service department of a company might follow to address complaints. The department can receive customer complaints in several ways: by phone, in person, or by email. Each of these represents a distinct starting point for the process. The department can resolve complaints several ways as well: the problem is fixed and the customer is satisfied, the problem can't be fixed and a refund is offered, or the problem is related to another department and the customer is transferred. These represent distinct outcomes.

A flow chart takes a process and makes its sequence visual. It provides instructions of how to go from point A to point B (or C or D) while removing much of the written or spoken language involved in giving such instructions. As you learned, anything visual is easier to digest, so flow charting makes processes easier to understand and follow, whether they have single or multiple starting points or outcomes.

Reading a Flow Chart

To understand how to read flow charts, it helps to understand how they are constructed. Flow charts are made of different shapes connected by lines. Each type of shape signifies a unique step or action. In the example below, diamonds are questions, rectangles are instructions, and rounded rectangles are the starting points and possible outcomes. Each shape is connected to the flow chart by at least one line, so to navigate the flow chart, you begin at the starting point and follow the line to the next shape or step. As you may have guessed, we're going to look at an example to illustrate.

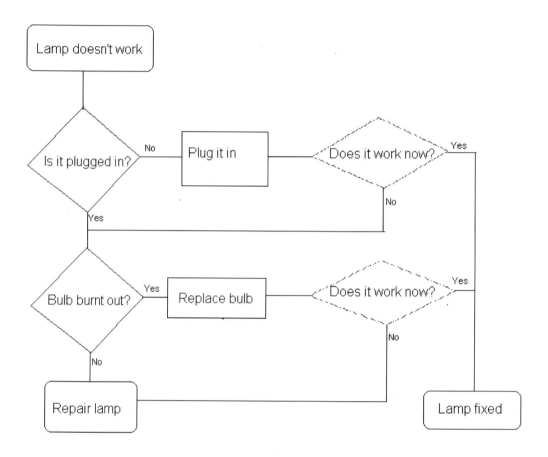

The flow chart diagram above displays the process of how to deal with a lamp that doesn't work. The starting point is *Lamp doesn't work*. This leads to the first question *Is it plugged in?* This question has two lines leading from it, one for each possible answer. The line for *no* leads to the instruction *Plug it in*. The line for *yes* leads to a new question.

Thus in following this diagram, you start by checking if it is plugged in. If it isn't plugged in, you follow the instruction to plug it in. This leads to the next question *Does it work now?* If the lamp works after you plug it in, then you are lead to the outcome – *Lamp fixed*. If it still doesn't work, you are lead to other instructions to follow.

All flow charts are read in this fashion. You begin at a starting point and navigate through lines and shapes based on the instructions and questions that are posed. At each step, you either follow the direction or answer the question. Then you follow the next line to the next step. In this way, you go through the remaining steps until you reach an outcome.

Reading a flow chart is not always as straightforward as the above example. The questions and choices in a flow chart can create a maze-like effect with a variety of overlapping and sometimes circular pathways. With more complex flow charts, especially those that are poorly designed, it is possible to get stuck in a loop or otherwise lost in the process. Let's look at how this may happen.

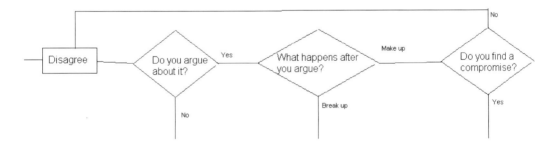

The above is a fragment of a larger flow chart that explores relationships. A decision made in another part of the chart leads to *Disagree*. This leads to a question *Do you argue?* If the answer is yes, then you are posed another question, *What happens after you argue?* The options offered include *Make up* or *Break up*. If you choose make up, it leads to a third question, *Do you find a compromise?* If you answer no, then you are right back to where you started with *Disagree*. If the same selections are made again, this loop will continue.

Flow charts are prone to this kind of circular loops. When creating your charts, be careful to avoid such loops. Programmers need to be especially careful when coding computer processes because these kinds of circular code can make a computer crash. If the situation forcing you into the loop is one you control, it's time to make new choices. If the situation forcing you into a loop is one out of your control, it's time to look for new options.

Overall, reading a flow chart is straightforward. Most flow charts do not have loops that trap a reader. If you are following a flow chart, you can read it in its entirety before beginning so you know what choices will lead you to an outcome you want. Let's take a look at ways you can use and apply flow charts.

Uses of Flow Charts

Flow charts can be used in many ways. They can be used to provide instructions, help make decisions, or illustrate a complex process. They can be included in manuals, procedures, websites, and many other places where they can help people visualize and better understand a process. We will discuss each use below.

Provide Instructions

The most popular use for flow charts is to provide instructions. Like the lamp example above, they can be used to provide a step-by-step guide on how to handle a task or complete a procedure. A person performing a task for the first time can easily comprehend the steps of a flow chart no matter how complex the procedure is or how many options they have. Flow chart instructions can also be used to help people identify the source of a problem.

Since flow charts can handle multiple decisions and multiple possibilities for each decision, they have a huge advantage over other forms of directives other than one-on-one communication. Written, video, or other forms of linear instructions become unwieldy when dealing with multiple choices. With these types of lessons, whenever a choice arises, determining where to address it becomes problematic: *If A, keep reading; if B, flip to page 44.* Someone who wants to select the second choice will need to go to a different part of the instructions. Worse, subsequent choices will lead to even more jumping around. This makes the instructions disjointed and difficult to follow. With a flow chart, no matter which choice a person selects, he or she can follow it without interruption all the way to the end.

Decision Making

Another popular use of flow charts is for decision making. Using flow charts to make decisions helps you to see and consider all conceivable outcomes at the same time. They show the advantages and disadvantages of each choice. They also allow you to see your thoughts on a decision. This is very helpful if your thoughts have been going around in circles. Getting the decision and your thoughts about it down in a flow chart can help you see where you are stuck and to help you break free.

Flow charts used for decision making are sometimes called *decision trees*. These trees start with a question, for instance *Should I go to college?* Off of this question would stem lines for two answers, *yes* and *no*. Starting with one answer, the person evaluating the decision explores all the possible outcomes. Selecting *yes* in this example could lead to outcomes like *leave home, more school, better jobs* and other things that would result from saying yes to going to college. Some of these results will lead to more questions or outcomes. For instance, *leave home* could lead to *live in a dorm, make new friends,* or *lose my significant other.* When every question and outcome of each choice is explored, the result can help one make a more informed decision.

Illustrate Complex Process

Still another use for the tool is to illustrate complicated processes. As you learned, flow charts can clearly show the various parts of a process and how everything flows from one part to another. This can prove useful in learning a variety of subjects. Areas as diverse as the animal food chain and politics deal with intricate procedures that need to be visualized to comprehend. A flow chart can help students visualize them, making it easier to learn and remember.

For example, if you were learning about the food chain, you might put together a flow chart like this:

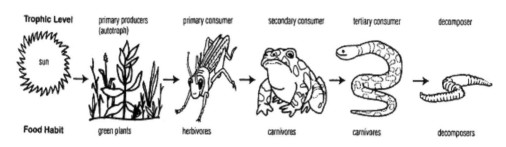

Source - Flint, M.L. and Gouveia P. 2001

Or if you wanted to be more descriptive, you might go with this diagram:

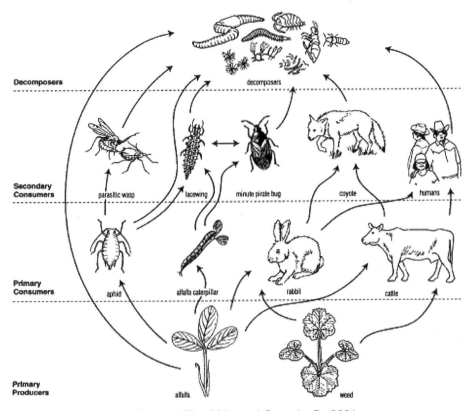

Source - Flint, M.L. and Gouveia, P. 2001

These diagrams show how microorganisms, insects, plants, and animals, both herbivores and carnivores, flow through the food chain. There is no need to read or hear a lengthy description. The process can be easily seen and thus easily understood and memorized.

Altogether, flow charts are very useful tools. They can be used in a wide variety of circumstances and benefit different types of people. Hopefully you've enjoyed this introduction. Let's now turn to concept maps.

CHAPTER 14 - CONCEPT MAPS

Concept maps explore the relationship between ideas. They represent visually how ideas interact and connect with each other. From this description, you are probably thinking, *isn't that what mind maps do?* Yes, but concept maps do it a little different and there is more hierarchy to them. In this chapter, you will find an introduction to concept maps, how to read them, and their uses and benefits.

What are Concept Maps?

There is a famous John Donne quote that says *No man is an island.* The point being made is that everyone is connected to other people in some fashion. It can also be said that no idea is an island. Every idea connects to other ideas in a web of meaning. When you learn a new idea, the idea is given meaning by how it connects to ideas you already understand.

Concept maps provide meaning to how ideas connect. They are made up of boxes or circles which hold ideas, and lines which describe the relationship between them. Each line has a verb or verb phrase which defines how the ideas relate. Below is a very simple concept map from the ecrp.uiuc.edu website to illustrate.

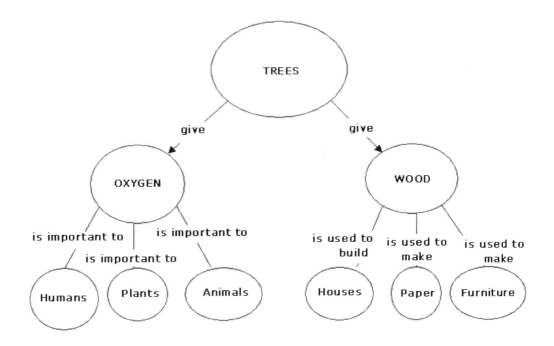

From the above, you see each concept map begins with a single idea. In this example, it is *Trees*. Trees points to two ideas, *Oxygen* and *Wood*, which are connected by a line with the verb *give*. These two ideas point to even more ideas. In this example, they are *Humans*, *Plants*, *Animals* and *Houses*, *Paper*, *Furniture*. This is a simple illustration of how concept maps are structured.

To more clearly understand its purpose and how to put one together, it helps to understand how they are read, which we discuss next.

Reading Concept Maps

Concept maps are designed to be read in a series of sentences. Two ideas and the verb or phrase that connects them make up one sentence. In the above example, we see that *Trees* is connected to *Oxygen*, and the line connecting them says *give*. This is read as *Trees give oxygen*. If you recall, from *Oxygen*, three more ideas emerge, *Humans*, *Plants*, and *Animals*. These ideas are connected with the phrase *is important to*. These would be read as *Oxygen is important to humans, Oxygen is important to plants*, and *Oxygen is important to animals*. These are the basics of reading concept maps.

Like a mind map, the ideas in a concept map are organized hierarchically. Unlike a mind map, where you start with the main idea in the center, with a concept map, the main idea starts at the top. This means ideas closer to the top of a concept map are broader and more general, and consequently, ideas towards the bottom are specific and more restricted. Therefore, a concept map is read by starting at the top and moving down to more and more specific ideas, all of which relate back to the top, most general idea.

Ideas are not inherently broad or specific. The situation in which they are considered determines, to a large extent, their meaning and application. For this reason, most concept maps are built around a pre-determined situation or question. Identifying the situation or question is one of the first steps to reading a concept map.

Similar to when reading a mind map, you should take a moment to skim a concept map before reading it. Identify the main idea, the most general idea that leads to all the other ideas. After skimming, you should be able to identify the situation or question the concept map is built around. For instance, anyone who reviews the sample concept map above should be able to tell that it is about the benefits of trees. If you can't identify the situation or the question a concept map is exploring, it is possible you missed something when skimming or the map may have been poorly constructed.

After skimming through the concept map and determining the situation or question it explores, go back to the top and read it in detail. The best way to do this is to read down a set of connections until you come to the end of one line. Then go back up and read along a different set of connections. Let's look at a more involved concept map to illustrate.

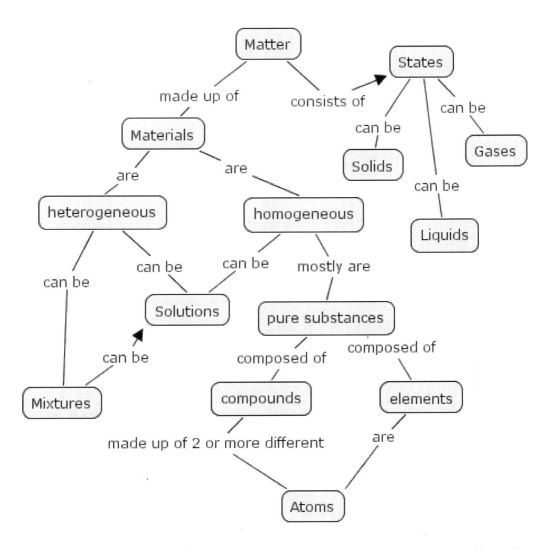

The above map, from the agpa.uakron.edu website, conceptualizes the scientific term *matter*. Since the main and most general concept is matter, it is placed at the peak. To read this, you might start with the connections: Matter → Materials → Heterogeneous → Mixtures. These set of connections would be read as *Matter is made up of materials. Materials are heterogeneous. Heterogeneous can be Mixtures.*

When you get to the end of one connection, you back up and follow another line of connections. In this case, you might instead back up one level and read Heterogeneous→Solutions, which is an alternative ending for this line of connections. This would be read *Heterogeneous can be solutions*.

By reading concept maps this way, you build a web of ideas in your mind, where each connected idea, as you think of it, leads to other ideas to which they are connected. Reading the connection Materials → Heterogeneous immediately tells your brain that this connection is closely related to the connection Materials → Homogeneous as they both stem from Material. Basically, the order in which you read the ideas tells your brain how closely related they are. Ideas which are read together will be remembered as being closely related. Ideas which are read with other ideas in between will be remembered as not being related, or being only distantly related.

The order is not the only important part of reading these diagrams. As you will learn in chapter 17, depending on the style of learner you are, the way you read them also affects how you remember them. A visual learner will benefit from focusing on the image of the concept map. An aural learner, from reading the map out loud. A kinesthetic learner, from tracing the connections between each idea. Again, you will learn more about this in a subsequent chapter.

This is how you read concept maps. It may take some getting used to because they are very different from the way ideas are normally explored. Once you are comfortable with them, though, they become very easy to review and understand.

Since you now understand how concept maps are read, you should also have a good grasp of how they are constructed. Use this knowledge when putting together your own diagrams. Start with the main thought or idea at the top. Then branch down to more specific ideas that are related to the top. With each branch, use a verb or verb phrase that communicates how the ideas are related. Keep going down into lower and lower-levels until you have noted everything.

Again, the above concept maps are fairly basic. We provided them to help you grasp the concept. You can go into considerable detail with your diagrams. Below is an example of just how intricate they can get.

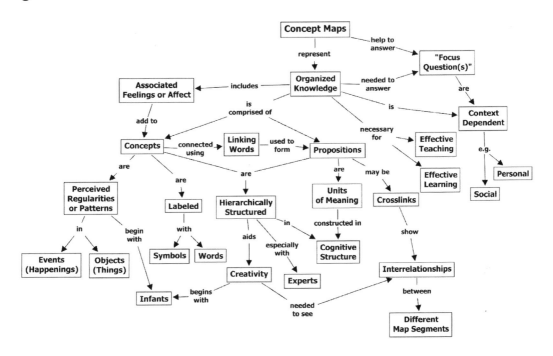

This concept map, from the *cmap.ihmc.us* website, is interestingly enough about concept mapping. Compared to the previous two, this one is much more elaborate. From this we can see that concept maps can handle complex topics and subjects.

Initially, this example may seem overwhelming, though it is not. Using the guidelines we set forth of following the connections one line at a time, you can tackle it quite easily. You start at the top with the phrase *Concept maps*. From there, you pick a line of connections, for instance the one going down the left side of the page: Concept maps → Organized knowledge → Concepts → Perceived regularities, and finally → Events (happenings). This is read as *Concepts maps represent organized knowledge. Organized knowledge is comprised of concepts*. And so on. Then you retreat to the top and go down the next line and then back up and down again and again.

Uses of Concept Maps

Concept maps are, first and foremost, learning tools. As such, there are easily dozens of ways they can be used to learn, teach, study, and explore ideas. There isn't room here to cover all their uses, but we will cover some of the more common ones. As a learning tool, they offer several benefits for both students and teachers. Like any tool, the benefits vary depending on the person and situation.

Note Taking

Like mind maps, concept maps can be used for note taking and organizing ideas from research, classes, or lectures. A concept map used for note taking begins with the overall topic on which you are taking notes. Like in our examples, other ideas are added below with connecting lines showing how they relate to the first idea and to each other.

Concept maps have a number of benefits for note taking. In general, they share most of the benefits of mind maps discussed earlier. Additionally, they better illustrate the complex relationships among ideas due to their descriptions in the connecting lines. They also show connections between multiple concepts, so that interactions between various concepts can be seen. The additional connections in a concept map, however, often make them seem less organized than a mind map.

Designing a Lesson or Syllabus

Many teachers will use concept maps as a tool for designing a lesson or syllabus. They will create a diagram based on the central idea of the course. They will then use it as a structural framework on which to build their teaching around, making sure to include all the ideas and connections on the map.

A lesson designed with a concept map can help students more fully understand an idea and all the related concepts. These lessons will improve the ability to convey the connections and relationships between ideas. Designing a lesson this way offers several benefits to the teacher as well. They can more easily ensure they are covering all the topics they need to, and they can use the connections between ideas to help them order those topics.

Evaluating Comprehension

Concept maps can be a wonderful tool for evaluating comprehension of a student. For example, making a concept map based on a student's essay can help both the student and teacher see how well the student understood his or her topic, how well the student conveyed the information, and any areas or connections a student may have missed or not explored as fully as he or she could have. This information can help the student understand consciously the relationship between ideas he or she has learned. It helps the teacher know in what areas the student needs help or where the weaknesses are in his or her knowledge.

Preserving Knowledge

Concept maps are not limited to classrooms. Corporations and other organizations make frequent use of the technique too. One popular business application is to preserve knowledge. Retiring or leaving employees are often asked to create concept maps to record their expertise. This way, a company doesn't lose important wisdom and subsequent employees can study and learn from the concept maps years after the expert has left.

The main benefit of using concept maps for preservation of knowledge is having that knowledge be easily accessible. The maps can be used in new employee training, by other experts looking for a different perspective on a problem, and in many other ways. A concept map of expert knowledge does not just provide facts, but also makes clear the way the expert connected those facts and ideas. This can help others gain a better understanding of systems and procedures the expert designed and help a replacement learn how that expert worked and what procedures and patterns he or she followed.

These are the ABCs of concept maps. It is a unique technique for visualizing relationships, which has uses both in education and business. Now that we've examined flow charts and concept maps, let's take a peek at the last relative of mind maps—cognitive mapping.

CHAPTER 15 - COGNITIVE MAPS

Unlike flow charts and concept maps, cognitive maps do not have a specific purpose. In fact cognitive maps do not have a specific anything. Cognitive mapping is a broad term for any map and can actually include mind maps and concept maps as well as many others. The vast majority of cognitive maps, however, are unique and don't follow the rules of other mapping techniques. Instead they are designed around the needs and preferences of the person making them and may combine elements of several mapping style.

Cognitive maps are to other mapping tools like stream of conscious writing is to a planned paper. With a cognitive map, you are exploring the associations within your own mind. You may start with one idea or several in order to look at how ideas relate or grow. Each idea you write down leads to another, which leads to another and another. Some new ideas connect back to old ideas. Some ideas lead to newer ideas. When you are done, you have a snapshot of how your mind understands or sees the topic you just mapped.

Uses of Cognitive Maps

The beautiful thing about cognitive maps is they can be used to illustrate almost anything you want. You can use a cognitive map to explore an idea, describe a relationship, plan a trip, or do anything else. Cognitive maps are incredibly open. As a general rule, any time you want to map something and none of the formal mapping methods such as mind maps, flow charts, or concept maps work for what you need, use a cognitive map.

All of this may sound vague. That is because cognitive maps can be used for so much and be done in so many different ways that it is not possible to give a really simple explanation that includes all the possibilities. Instead of a formal instruction, therefore, you'll find three examples used to illustrate possible ways to make, read, and use a cognitive map.

Mapping Relationships

As indicated, cognitive maps don't need to start with a single idea. They can start with as many central points as needed. This means a cognitive map can be used to illustrate relationships between people, corporations, countries, and many other topics. As an example, let's take a look at a cognitive map of the relationships in a family.

Ann and Adam are wife and husband. Anne is the mother of Jen and Joe, and Adam is their father. Jen and Joe are brother and sister. Ann is an artist and has been teaching Joe, so they also relate as teacher and student. We can point out other relationships among the family, but this is enough to get started. All of these complex relationships among the family can be illustrated in the map below.

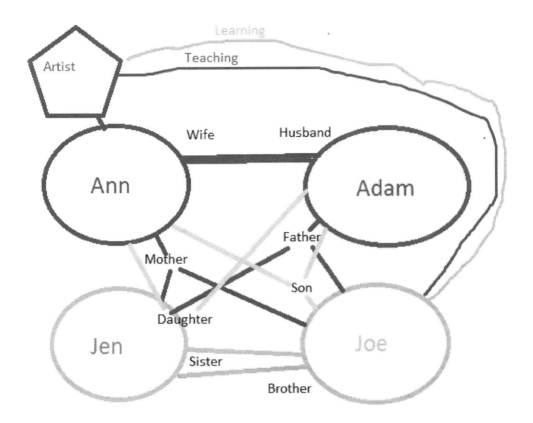

With this map, we started not with one central point, but four. The four points are represented by each member of the family—Ann, Adam, Jen, and Joe. From there we created lines to show the relationships between them. We also included a specific aspect of one of the family members, Ann as an artist.

This kind of cognitive map is more complicated than any other type of map we've looked at so far. Relationships are very complicated things. As a result, reading a map like this can also be complicated. The best way to approach reading this map is to start with one person in the family and read all of his or her connections. Then move to another family member and read all of their connections. Repeat this until you have read all the connections of each individual. Reading the map in this way makes each member of the relationship the central figure for their part of the map.

These types of relationship maps may be most useful for family therapists and counselors. Therapists can use a cognitive map of the relationships to explore the major players in a family and what the healthy and unhealthy areas of each player might be and what changes would benefit everyone involved.

Cognitive maps of other types of relationships can be used in other ways. A cognitive map of the relationship between countries may be useful for a student studying history. A corporation considering an international expansion may wish to see how the laws of the countries they are operating in will interact and affect that company. The trade relationship between countries would also make a useful cognitive map for economists. Can you think of other uses for a cognitive map illustrating the relationship between different countries?

Very complicated cognitive maps are used in biology and medicine. The relationships between different animals and organisms in an environment can be illustrated with a cognitive map to explore the ecology of an area. Diagrams of the metabolism are cognitive maps illustrating a process far too complex to be easily explained. A metabolic cognitive map often shows the relationship between dozens of hormones, enzymes, and nutrients.

Exploring Stream of Conscious

Cognitive maps can also be used to record stream-of-conscious thoughts. Take a look at the example cognitive map below. An author, David, has an idea for a story. He has decided to explore the idea through a cognitive map. Since it is only the beginning of a story, he's decided to build the cognitive map in a stream of conscious fashion. This will allow him to explore the idea fully without worrying about organization or logic. That will come later.

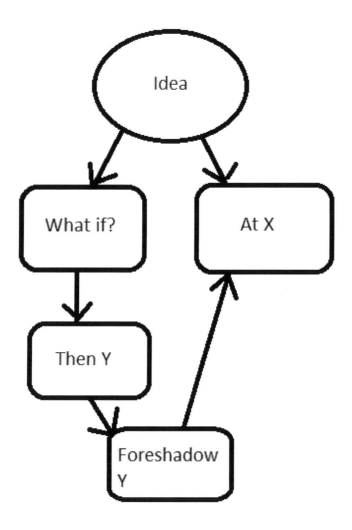

His initial idea leads to two thoughts, *what if this happens* and *the story's setting at X*. He doesn't have any further thoughts for setting, but the *what if* leads to a *then Y happens* and now David has an idea for how to foreshadow *Y*. The foreshadowing will connect back to the setting, because the description of the setting will be an important part of foreshadowing. This continues, with each thought leading to a new thought in a somewhat random and unpredictable fashion. Each thought is added to the cognitive map and connected to any and all other ideas to which it relates.

When David's map is finished, he will have fully expanded and explored his initial idea, and all the thoughts it brings to mind. Some of these thoughts will be completely unrelated or dead ends that don't work with the story even though they are related to the initial idea. When David is ready, he will go through the cognitive map and decide which ideas to include and which to discard. He may create a new, organized map using only the ideas and thoughts that he chose to include.

Reading stream of conscious cognitive maps is often chaotic and may be confusing. Our minds tend to make strange connections and jumps between ideas, and when we are recording thoughts as they come, all of those jumps and connections will appear in the map. Stream of conscious cognitive maps can best be read by following the flow of ideas without forcing any specific direction. If your eye is drawn to the left branch, follow the left branch. If you're drawn to a connection jumping across the page, by all means, jump across the page. Do not try and impose an order or organization on these maps.

Stream of conscious cognitive maps can be used for many things besides creative brainstorming. As a teaching tool, they can help a student explore their personal understanding of a subject and how that subject connects to seemingly unrelated topics. A business person might use a stream of conscious cognitive map to help him or her think through all the numerous aspects of a business proposal.

They can also be used in therapy to explore ideas and associations of which a person isn't fully aware. By making a stream of conscious map, a person can see and understand their thoughts, including subconscious thoughts of which they weren't fully aware before. By making otherwise hidden thoughts visible, a person making this type of map can explore his or her own psyche, brainstorm an idea, work through an emotional reaction to a suggestion, and much more. The use of the technique offers a better understanding of the thoughts and ideas in one's own mind and clearer thinking that comes from exposing hidden connections and associations to conscious awareness.

Incorporating Multimedia

While cognitive maps are traditionally built around words, and more rarely, pictures, there is no reason they can't be made with a wide variety of media. Especially with computer support, cognitive maps can be made with sound clips, images, even video. As an example, let's consider a couple planning their wedding.

The couple decides to use a cognitive map as a way to record their thoughts and ideas about what they want for their wedding. Using a computer program, they create a cognitive map which includes links to websites for wedding planners with whom they are going to interview, pictures of possible locations, notes on vows, images and descriptions of possible themes, and sound clips of songs they are debating for the wedding and reception.

As time goes on, they may remove some things from the cognitive map—for instance, the audio clip of a song they have decided not to use. Other things can be added—a scanned image of their invitations or a link to their wedding registry. Their cognitive map becomes a place where everything about their wedding can come together. It lets them see, hear, and consider every aspect of their plans and desires.

Multimedia cognitive maps aren't necessarily read. They are watched, listened to, clicked, and explored. A multimedia cognitive map can be as much visual and aural as verbal. Each map will be absorbed differently, depending on how the creator chose to organize it, but in general, you will want to start at the central point(s) and explore outward.

Often a multimedia map is not explored all at once. In our example, the happy couple will probably look at a specific section of their cognitive map—for instance, possible locations or theme ideas—to discuss that specific section more often than they will look over the entire map. Of course, they will want to explore the whole map from time to time, both to make sure everything is working in harmony and just for the pleasure of watching their wedding come together.

The multi-sensory nature of a multimedia cognitive map makes it a great tool for planning many kinds of events. Everything from major conferences and conventions to family reunions and class parties can be planned and put together using this tool. With some mapping programs, it is even possible for multiple people to use multiple computers to build a multimedia map together over the internet.

Another way to use a multimedia cognitive map is to make a record of an event. For instance, after the wedding, our newlyweds might use clips from the video of their wedding, the music they danced to, pictures taken by guests, and much more to create a summary cognitive map of their wedding as it happened. This can provide a source of happy memories for the couple and a way to share their special day with people who may not have been able to attend.

Multimedia cognitive maps' use go beyond events. A student who learns best with visual aids might use multimedia in a cognitive map for studying. An architect might combine video of an existing location, personal notes, and sketches of possible designs to build a multimedia cognitive map for a renovation or other building project.

The benefits of using multimedia in cognitive maps are the same no matter what your purpose may be. By including multimedia, you incorporate other senses into the diagram. In this way, you are able to engage multiple areas of the brain in planning, studying, and remembering the essential details. The use of multimedia provides a fuller understanding of the goals of the map, especially when the cognitive map is being used to depict something that is three dimensional and real, not mere words on a page.

This ends our discussion of cognitive maps. As you can see, they take a wide variety of forms. The greatest strength of cognitive mapping is its flexibility. They can be molded to fit any style and fill any purpose you can imagine. This flexibility can also be a weakness as cognitive maps are often less organized than other types of maps. This can cause others to have more difficulty reading and understanding them, especially if the cognitive map is complex, with no clear starting point. Cognitive maps aren't the tool for every purpose, but for many purposes that other mapping tools don't meet, such as relationships, stream of consciousness, or employing multimedia, cognitive maps can be very useful and beneficial.

Wrapping Up

In this section, you were introduced to the close cousins of mind mapping—flow charts, concept maps, and cognitive maps. Each of these tools have their strengths. Flow charts are wonderful for recording and learning processes, especially a process where there are multiple options and end points. Concept maps explore ideas and how they relate to other ideas, creating an understanding of how concepts interact with each other. Cognitive maps are infinitely flexible and may be used for any imaginable purpose.

In comparison, mind maps have some of the flexibility of cognitive maps, being useful for a wide variety of purposes, but are far more organized. They lack the cross connections of concept maps, but have a clear hierarchy that shows how everything relates to a single specific idea. Mind maps tend to lack any sort of flow, so their structure does not lend to describing a process.

Nonetheless, since flow charts, concept maps, and cognitive maps are all visual tools and have a diagram like structure, you can combine or integrate them into a mind map. Like a cognitive map, you might start out not with a single idea in the center, but rather four ideas. From the center, you would branch outward with each idea. One idea would branch top left, another top right, another bottom left, and the last, bottom right. And instead of having empty or static branches, you might borrow the pattern from a concept map or flow chart. One set of branches might have a verb or verb phrase describing the connections. Another set of branches would employ arrows to describe a flow or process. By borrowing aspects of the other three techniques, you can develop very advanced mind maps.

Hopefully you have enjoyed meeting these relatives of mind mapping. All of them can be useful and enjoyable tools in the right circumstance. In the next section, we revert to the discussion of mind mapping, but as it relates to children.

SECTION V

MIND MAPPING AND CHILDREN

So far this book has focused on mind maps as a resource for adults. They are also a valuable aid to children-of almost any age. In this section, you will learn some of the benefits mind maps offer children, discover which children gain the most from using mind maps, learn how to teach them the system, and get a peek at how even very young children can apply the technique. We will start this section with benefits.

CHAPTER 16 - MIND MAPPING FOR CHILDREN

Adults tend to experience difficulty adjusting to mind mapping. After a lifetime of linear thinking, it can take effort to think associatively. As a result, it can take an adult a while to catch on and become comfortable with the associative nature of mind mapping.

Children, on the other hand, have a much easier time. They are still learning to think linearly, so associative thinking comes naturally to them. Recall how hard it can be to get children to stay *on topic*. They tend to be all over the place. One thought leads to another, and another, and another, until you can barely keep up. Children's ease with associations makes them great candidates for mind maps.

One of the main benefits mind mapping offers children is that it helps them sort their thinking. Children don't deal well with abstract ideas, but as you have learned, mind maps bring abstract concepts into concrete form. They present ideas visually, so children can concretely see the various connections. Seeing the associations and connections assists children in recognizing how their thoughts can be arranged.

Once children learn mind mapping, it can be a great tool for them both in school and at home. They can use mind maps to take notes of text books, study for a test, and plan school projects. At home, a mind map can be a big help in keeping up with chores and household responsibilities. Children will find it easier to remember their chores if they organize them with a to-do list mind map rather than with a traditional to-do list.

Teaching Children Mind Mapping

With the right guidance, children can learn mind mapping rather quickly. All they need is a teacher who is familiar with mind maps and can explain them in a way children will understand. With a bit of practice, they will pick up the basics without any problems.

Children will learn mind maps more easily if they are able to make one or see one being made. As mentioned, children do not grasp abstract concepts. If you try to explain what a mind map is, they won't understand as easily as they will if they have a picture of a mind map in front of them. Even more, they will understand the steps of making a mind map more clearly if they can see it happen. Watching a mind map come together helps children understand what they are and how to make them.

To begin, let's go over a step-by-step lesson you can use to teach any child this technique. After the lesson, you'll find several suggestions for adapting the lesson for young children.

Step-by-Step Mind Mapping Lesson

Step 1 – Prepare for the lesson. There are three parts to preparation: planning what you will say and do, gathering the materials you need, and finding time that you and the child(ren) have to sit down together. Preparation makes teaching easier. It prevents running around at the last minute trying to find pens and paper. Also, it helps you explain mind maps more effortlessly and without the need to stop to figure out what words to use.

Planning what you will say and do is similar to planning any other presentation. Read over this lesson several times to make sure you are familiar with all the steps. It might help to make a mind map of the lesson, with subheadings of things you need to tell the children or demonstrate for them. Make sure you are comfortable with mind maps yourself and familiar with the concepts behind them before introducing it to children.

As part of your plan, take a look over your child's upcoming school work and activities. You can use their work or activity as a basis for your map. Doing so will give your child better perspective on the technique. If your child has a book report, science paper, or other school project coming up, you can plan to teach your child mind mapping using that project as a topic for their mind map.

If your child doesn't have an upcoming school project, think about what he or she enjoys doing with respect to the various uses of mind maps discussed in the earlier section. If your child likes to tell stories, you can show him or her how to use a mind map to develop and write a story. If he or she has trouble remembering assignments or chores, show them a to-do list mind map. A brainstorm mind map can also be helpful for a child who has trouble finding things to do on rainy days. Figure out how your child might employ mind maps, and use that as a platform for your lesson.

Gathering materials should be simple. You will want this lesson to refer to (or a mind map of it), several sheets of paper, writing instruments in a variety of colors, and a flat surface on which to work. If your child has special pens or pencils he or she enjoys using, try and use those. Once you gather all the materials, you are almost ready to begin.

As it relates to time, finding a moment to teach mind mapping will be either simple or a bit of a challenge. If you are a working parent whose children are in after school activities, this can create difficulty. On the other hand, if you are a stay-at-home mom or dad whose children usually have a few hours of quiet time during the afternoons, fitting in mind maps should be fairly simple. If you have difficulty finding time during the weekday, you might choose to schedule a weekend or rainy day.

Step 2—Get started. Sit down with your child and your materials. Explain mind maps briefly and without getting into detail. *Mind maps* *are a tool for organizing your thoughts* or *Mind maps are a way to explore an idea.* Keep it simple and relevant.

Use this explanation as a lead-in to what you will be doing. Tell your children that you will be showing them how to make a mind map, and what you can use a mind map for. *I want to show you how you can make a mind map to help you write your report* or *I know you're interested in cars, so we're going to use a mind map to learn more about them.* Again, keep it simple.

Step 3—Make the mind map. Get out your piece of paper and have your child pick out a pen or pencil with which to write. Tell them that every mind map is built around a main topic or main idea. For your map, you'll be using the topic you told your child that you'd be discussing. From the above examples, the main topic would either be the topic of the child's report or cars. Have your child write this topic in the center of the paper and circle it.

Now it's time to discuss subtopics. You can start with something like *The next layer of the mind map is made up of things about (the main topic) that are important. What do you think are some important things about (the main topic)?* Discuss the children's ideas and make some suggestions of your own. They can come up with as many subtopics they want, but encourage them to have at least two. When they are done, tell them that these important things are called subtopics.

A discussion about subtopics for cars might go like this:

Parent: We want to come up with some questions about cars, but we want them to be specific. So before we start thinking about questions, let's come up with some things about cars that are important.

Child: Like how they work?

172

Parent: Sure, how cars work is pretty important. Go ahead and write that down on the paper. Then draw a line from *Cars* in the middle to *how cars work*. Can you think of any others?

Child: How about *what cars are made of*.

Parent: That sounds good too. Write it down on the other side of the paper from *how cars work* and draw a line to *Car*. Any other ideas?

Child: I want to learn about people who make cars—is that still about cars?

Parent: I think so. Let's add that too. How about you write that one at the bottom of the paper. Do you want to add another important thing?

Child: No, I can't think of anything. Can you?

Parent: What about the different types of cars, is that important?

Child: Well, yeah. I'll put that at the top.

While you are discussing the subtopics, you can tell them about the use of different shapes and different colors. *Using different colors and different shapes helps you see different ideas right away. You can pick any color or shape you want for the separate parts of the mind map.*

Depending on the child's preference, he or she might make all the subtopics the same color and shape or make them all different colors and different shapes. They may not be able to explain why they are doing it that way, but let them set it up the way they want. Whether they can explain it or not, their choices will have meaning for them, a meaning that relates to the ideas they are writing down.

Different main topics would lead to a slightly different approach to subtopics. For a book report you might ask *What are some important things about the book you want to talk about in your report?* Some children will have an easier time understanding if you say *big things* rather than *important things*—small details can be important, but they aren't subtopics.

Lower-level topics are discussed in much the same way you discussed subtopics. Starting with the first subtopic, ask *What are some specific things about (the subtopic) that you want to (include in your report/learn/try/etc.)?* Continuing with the car example, you could ask, *What are some questions about how cars work that you want to ask?* Answers might be things like *What makes them move? How do they turn?* or (for the real car enthusiast) *How are they wired?* Have them write their ideas down with lines connecting to the subtopic.

Some children are quiet or shy and don't like to volunteer ideas. If yours are like this, you'll need to work to engage them and bring them into the discussion. You might do this by making suggestions for sub and lower-level topics and either asking their opinion or asking if they will take turns making suggestions. Another alternative is to not discuss anything at all. Instead of having a discussion, you can just tell them to write down the important or specific things they think up.

Once all the lower-level branches are added, the mind map is complete. Read it over with your child. Ask them if they want to make any changes. If they are happy with the end result, you are ready to go on to the next step.

Step 4—Use the mind map. Application is everything. After the mind map is finished, you'll want to show the children how to use it. How they use it will depend on their initial reason for creating it. A brainstorm mind map that generates ideas about what to do on a rainy day is easy to use. They can pick the idea they like best and go have fun. The car mind map example can be taken to the library, computer, or book store to look up answers to the questions.

A mind map made to organize a book report is a bit more complicated. For something like this, your child will start by picking the order they will write the subtopics. Then he or she will write about each subtopic in that order, checking off branches as they are discussed. After all the subtopics have been written, have your child write an introduction and conclusion at the beginning and end of the piece. (For more details on using a mind map for a writing project, see *Writing Non-Fiction* in chapter 7).

Young Children and Mind Maps

Young children (what schools call *pre-readers* and *early readers*) cannot make or read mind maps for themselves because either they do not know or are just learning how to read and write. Nonetheless, they can still use mind mapping and learn from them. The technique can be used as a training wheel of sorts to jump start their early education.

Since young children can't read mind maps, you can make them with pictures. Mind maps made with pictures are perfect for young adolescents. The young respond very well to pictures and images—that's why picture books are so popular and have been the main form of content in children's books over the past half century. A mind map made with pictures provides information in a form that they can understand (pictures) and in a way that makes sense to them (associative). Combining the two is very effective with young children.

How do you make a mind map with pictures? Let's consider a mother who is helping her young daughter learn shapes before entering kindergarten. In the middle of the paper, as the main topic, she writes the word *Shapes*. As subtopics, she draws pictures of the most common shapes—*circle, square, rectangle, triangle,* and *oval*. Then as lower level topics, she draws variations of each shape—different sizes, colors, and dimensions. So off of *rectangle*, she will have a tall green rectangle, a short wide blue rectangle, and a small red rectangle.

She can put this on the wall for her daughter to see and look at, and when they talk about shapes, she can take it down and read over it with her, helping her learn the names of the shapes.

Not all topics can be made into pictures as easily as shapes. However, young children focus on concrete ideas, so you should be able to find some picture for almost any topic you'd be mind mapping for a young child. For instance, for a chores mind map, you might take a photograph of the child doing the chores or cut out such pictures from a magazine. You might even ask the child to suggest pictures for different ideas. This will get him or her involved in the mind mapping process.

This covers introducing mind maps to children, including young children. Of course, not all children learn the same way, so you may need to adapt the lesson to the learning style of your child. Let's look at some of the different learning styles and how to gear mind map lessons to them.

CHAPTER 17 - TEACHING MIND MAPS FOR DIFFERENT LEARNING STYLES

There are four main learning styles: visual, verbal, aural, and kinesthetic. Visual learners are those who learn by seeing. They pick up information through pictures, diagrams, and by watching things happen. Verbal learners learn best through words. Outlines and other traditional organizational tools work very well for these types of people. Aural learners learn through hearing. They learn best when they are told what to do and how. One-on-one instructions, lectures, and presentations are the hallmark of this style. Kinesthetic learners, on the other hand, learn by doing. For these learners, you can tell and/or show them what to do, but the information will internalize only when they do it on their own. These are the four learning styles.

A child's learning style determines how receptive a child will be to mind maps. When teaching children mind maps, you will want to adapt your lesson to suit the learning style of the child or children you are working with. Children learn best when lessons match the way they learn. Here a few ways to adapt your lessons for the different learning styles.

Visual Mind Map Lessons

One of the best things you can do to help a visual learner understand mind maps is to have a sample mind map prepared before you begin the lesson. Make sure the sample mind map contains a mix of colors, shapes, and possible sketches. Show the visual learner the sample and how everything connects. Give him or her time to examine the mind map and become familiar with it. Explain the different levels of the mind map and the meaning of different shapes and colors. In seeing the example first, the visual learner is able to understand what a mind map is and what it is supposed to look like before he or she begins making one on his or her own.

In addition to showing a visual learner a mind map, it will also help if you make a mind map while the learner watches. A visual learner can learn how to make a mind map by watching you make yours. If visual learners can see exactly how the mind map is constructed and how everything comes together. Then when they make their own, they are practicing what they have visually seen.

When your visual learners are making their own mind maps, encourage them to use colors, shapes, and sketches. The more visually interesting their diagram is, the more useful it will be for them. They will have an easier time recognizing and recalling the ideas in the map. Some highly visual learners can make mind maps entirely out of sketches, using a symbol or drawing to indicate each idea.

Aural Mind Map Lessons

A sample mind map can also help aural learners understand mind maps. In this case, the sample becomes a cue card for you and the child. You should name each piece of the mind map. Point out and describe the connections between the main topic, subtopics, and lower-level topics. Aural learners need to hear to fully absorb information, so make sure to tell them everything you want them to know about mind maps.

As your aural learners make their own mind maps, describe what they are doing at each step. For instance, while they are writing down a subtopic you could say, *Drawing a line between the subtopic and main topic shows that they are connected.* When they are finished, have them read their maps out loud so they can hear themselves and learn from the sound of their own voices as well.

Verbal Mind Map Lessons

Verbal learners absorb information best in the form of words. Most verbal learners are also aural learners—they learn better either from reading written words or hearing spoken words. For a verbal learner, it is best to begin with a sample mind with all the sections properly labeled. Label the main topic *main topic*, label each of the subtopics *subtopic*, and label the lines between the different ideas *connection* and so on. Let the verbal learner see the words that define and describe a mind map, and then explain each part of the mind map the way you would for an aural learner.

When a verbal learner is making their own mind map, have them explain what they are doing as they work. As they write down the main topic, they can say *this is the main topic, it's the central idea of the mind map*. If they use different colors or different shapes, ask them what those colors and shapes mean. *The circle means that this is the main topic, I'm going to use squares for the subtopics.* (Don't expect them to explain why they are using circle for main topic and square for subtopic).

Kinesthetic Mind Map Lessons

Kinesthetic learners tend to be in a very different position in school. These students learn by doing, and their style of learning is rarely emphasized in an educational system where children are told to sit, watch, and listen all day. Mind maps help these students by adding a physical component to learning. When teaching kinesthetic learners, keep your explanations brief and let them begin making their mind maps as soon as possible. Guide them through it the way the step-by-step mind map lesson describes in the previous chapter. Kinesthetic learners will understand mind maps after making one themselves.

After making a mind map, have the kinesthetic learners trace it. Tracing over the map—either with a pen or their finger—lets them act out the connections and relationships between different ideas. This motion is akin to performing a physical action and so will help them learn their material in a way that outlines and other learning tools can't match. When tracing a mind map, it also helps if a kinesthetic learner reads it out loud. Reading out loud, interestingly enough, is another form of doing. It connects the feel and shape of their mouth speaking the words. Both the action of tracing the mind map and reading it out loud will help this type of learner remember how the ideas connect.

Teaching for Multiple Learning Styles

If you are teaching more than one child, such as in school or a classroom, it is likely you will be dealing with a variety of learning styles. In this case, you'll want to combine different styles to get the best results for each child. For example, a kinesthetic learner can trace and read a sample mind map while a visual learner will learn from watching the tracing and reading of it. An aural learner learns by listening to the kinesthetic learner read. Teaching children with a variety of learning styles can be a challenge, but it is possible with some forethought and planning.

When teaching multiple children, it is best if you know ahead of time what each child's learning style is. Knowing this in advance allows you to plan for the different learning styles with which you will be dealing. For instance, if you know you will be teaching a mix of kinesthetic and visual learners, you don't need to worry about adapting your lesson to aural learners. Simply gear the instructions for these two leaning types. Allow the learning styles of your students to dictate your lesson plan.

To prepare a mind mapping lesson for children with multiple learning styles, pick out at least one adaptation for each learning style you expect to be teaching. Build your lesson plan to include each of these adaptations. In this way, all the children you are teaching will be able to learn about mind maps in the way that works best for them.

If you don't know ahead of time what the children's learning styles are, you can still teach them mind mapping. Just prepare a lesson plan for all four styles of learning. Start with one style. If none of the students respond to the approach, move onto the next one. Keep switching until you find a style to which the children respond.

These are the four main learning styles—visual, aural, verbal, and kinesthetic. By gearing your mind map lessons to one of these styles, you make it easier and more fun for children to grasp the technique. In fact, this approach can be used to make almost any subject easier and more fun to learn. You might even apply the information in this chapter to identify your learning style, and gear your own studies towards it. In the next chapter, we will cover ways to incorporate mind maps into your child's life.

CHAPTER 18 - USING MIND MAPS AS LEARNING ACTIVITIES AND AROUND THE HOME

So far this section has focused on introducing mind maps to children and leveraging children's learning styles when teaching them the technique. This chapter takes you one step further to show you the different ways to incorporate mind maps into your child's life. At the start, we mentioned that children can use mind maps both as a learning tool and at home with various chores and responsibilities. This chapter will expand on these two areas.

Using Mind Maps as Learning Activities

One way to get your child mind mapping is to integrate the activity into his or her learning. In the beginning of this section, we described how to teach a child about the different types of shapes with a picture mind map. This is a perfect example of using mind maps for learning activities with young children.

At one time, children were expected to learn their alphabet, shapes, and numbers in kindergarten. Now, in many parts of the country, they are expected to have this knowledge before they start kindergarten so that their teachers can go directly into reading and writing. Mind maps can help young children learn the essentials so they can start kindergarten ready to go.

There are several ways to use mind maps to help young children learn. Let's take a look at some of these ways and how they can be used to help children learn.

Numbers Mind Map

A numbers mind map is easy to make and can help young children learn to count to 10. Put *Numbers* as the main topic. Each number from 1-10 will be a subtopic. Write the numeral and the name of the number. For the next level, use groups of objects. For instance, under the subtopic *1*, you could have two lower-level topics: a picture of 1 apple and a picture of 1 tree. Then under subtopic *2*, you could have 2 apples and 2 trees, and so on.

You can make this mind map yourself, or you can have your child help you make it. If you decide to let your child help, start by writing the main topic and subtopics on the paper. Next you have a few options. Your child can count while you draw the lower-level branches, or you can have your child draw them, or if you are feeling adventurous, your child can glue or tape beads, cereal O's, or other small counters to represent lower-level branches. If your young child helps make the mind map, then the process in of itself becomes a learning activity.

Shape Mind Map

The example in chapter 16 under *Young Children and Mind Maps* describes one way to make a shape mind map. If you'd like, you could have your child help make it in a fashion similar to the process described in the numbers mind map subsection above. If the child doesn't have the fine motor skills to draw shapes yet, he or she can find pictures of shapes in magazines that you can cut out for them to glue on to the map.

Alphabet Mind Map

There are several ways that you can make mind maps about the alphabet. If you have a big enough piece of paper, you can make a mind map of the entire alphabet. If your child is proficient in the alphabet, you can make a vowel and consonants mind map or a vowel sounds mind map.

To make an alphabet mind map, write *ABCs* or *Alphabet* as the main topic. Then make each of the letters a subtopic (make sure you use a big piece of paper). Each subtopic should have the capital and lowercase letter. Then for lower-level topics, put pictures of things which begin with that letter. Your child will have extra fun if you can personalize the mind map. For instance, if your young child has an aunt, use her picture under *A* (Aunt Joan). If you have a dog, put a picture of your dog under *D*. As with a shape or number mind map, your child can help you make this mind map or you can make it yourself and read it with them.

A child who already knows the alphabet can still learn a great deal about letters from a mind map. A vowel and consonants mind map shows the distinction between the two. It begins with two subtopics— vowels and consonants. Under vowels, the lower-level branches are *A, E, I, O* and *U*. Everything else goes under consonants.

Lastly, a vowel sounds mind map can help young learners prepare for reading. *Vowels* will be your main topic, with each vowel as a subtopic. For lower-level topics, use words and pictures that illustrate the different vowel sounds. For instance, with E you could use *net* and *tree*. This kind of alphabet mind map shows children how letters function in words and basic phonics rules, paving the way for reading.

Early Reader Mind Map

If your child is ready to start reading simple words, early reader mind maps can help him or her get started. This type of diagram is based around a topic that is familiar to your child, such as people or animals.

For instance, you might make an early reader mind map with the main topic *people*. Subtopics could be *family, friends,* and *everyone*. Under family, add lower-level topics for *Dad* (with a picture of Dad), *Mom* (with a picture of Mom) and so on. Within this branch, you can include just your immediate family or extended family such as *Aunt,*

Uncle, etc. Under *friends*, add lower-level topics for your child's friends, your neighbors, as well as close family friends. For the subtopic *Everyone*, you can list everybody else, such as the president, your child's favorite television character, even the mail man.

An early reader mind map helps a child become familiar with common words related to the topic of the mind map. You could create early reader mind maps about any number of topics with every new map introducing more words for your child to learn.

As you have seen, children can benefit in several ways from mind maps. As a bonus, children introduced to mind maps at a young age will learn to make and use mind maps through your example. When they are older, they will know how to create mind maps for their own needs and projects.

Using Mind Maps around the Home

Using mind maps around the home helps children understand what is happening and what they are supposed to do. They can help children learn the regular schedule of your household and help them adjust to sudden schedule changes—for instance, when the holidays throw routines upside down. Below you will find three examples of using mind maps with children around the house—a chores mind map, a schedule mind map, and a holiday mind map.

Chores Mind Map

Most children have a few chores around the house for which they are responsible. These include anything from tidying up their room, putting dirty clothes in the laundry basket, and carrying their dishes into the kitchen after meals. To help them remember these chores, you could put up a list on the wall, regularly ask and remind your child about them, or you could create a picture mind map.

Let's consider Martha and her son Dan. Dan is 5 and in kindergarten. He has things he needs to do before he goes to school in the morning and things he needs to do at night before he goes to bed. Martha creates a picture mind map so he will be able to see what needs to be done each day.

In the center of the page, Martha puts a picture of Dan and writes *Dan's To-do List*. Dan is learning to read, so labeling the pictures will help him learn. Martha makes two subtopics, *morning* and *evening*. For morning she uses a picture of sunrise, for evening a picture of sunset.

Lower-level topics for morning are brushing his teeth, eating breakfast, and making his bed. She uses pictures of a toothbrush, a bowl of cereal, and his bed. Lower-level topics for evening are doing homework, eating dinner, having a bath, and brushing his teeth again. For homework she uses a picture of Dan doing his homework, for dinner a picture of a hamburger, and for bath a picture of a bath toy.

She can get pictures from magazines, by taking them with a camera, or by drawing them herself. When she is done, she has a picture mind map of what Dan needs to do each day. If she wants, she can make copies of the mind map, so Dan has one for each day. Then he can check off things as he completes them.

Obviously each family is different and different children will have different things on their to-do list for each day. The same basic process should work for everyone. Divide the things to be done into groups—Martha used time of day, but they can just as easily be divided by room where they are done or day of the week. Then create the map, making sure to incorporate pictures as much as possible. Next we take a look at using mind maps to help a child understand a holiday schedule.

Schedule Mind Map

Children are comfortable with routine. It helps them feel safe knowing what is going on and when. As exciting and fun as holidays are, they can disrupt children's routine. The schedule upset caused by holidays can prevent children from knowing what is going on or what they are supposed to be doing. Creating a mind map of the holiday schedule can help children better handle the changes so they can enjoy the holidays without being confused.

Melissa and John have two children, Peggy and Rob. Peggy is 4 and Rob is 6. Last Christmas, Rob spent the whole day asking when things were going to happen –*When can I open my presents*? *When is Granma coming*? *When is dinner*? *When is everyone leaving*? This year, Melissa and John decided to create a mind map to show Rob the schedule of events. With a bit of luck, Rob will even be able to use the diagram to answer questions her sister Peggy asks!

Melissa and John put a picture of a Christmas tree in the center of their mind map. Than for subtopics, they put pictures of a clock at different times of the day. Rob is learning to read clocks in school, and if he isn't sure, he can look at the real clock in his room and see if it matches the pictures.

The family will have breakfast at 8 am. They will open presents at 9. Then the children will have time to play until Granma comes at 3 pm. Dinner will be at 5 pm, and bedtime at 7. So Melissa and John have five clock faces on their mind map: *8:00, 9:00, 3:00, 5:00* and *7:00*. Each clock face subtopic will have only one lower-level branch—the activity for that hour. *8:00* has a bowl of cereal, *9:00* a picture of a wrapped gift, *3:00* a picture of Granma, *5:00* a picture of dinner and *7:00* a picture of bed. Throughout the day, when Rob asks when something will occur, Melissa and John can have him refer to his mind map.

Holiday Mind Map

Holidays can be confusing for children in other ways. Some holidays have rules that are different from regular days, like giving up something for Lent, fasting during Ramadan, or avoiding bread during Passover. Sometimes these rules are fairly straightforward, but not always. A mind map can help young children remember how the holiday routine is different.

Rebecca and Joseph keep Passover every year for the full 8 days. Their young children have a lot of favorite foods that they can't eat during this time—like hamburgers. This year, to help their children remember what they can and can't eat, Rebecca and Joseph make a picture mind map. The main topic is *Passover foods*. They make two subtopics: *Foods to Eat* and *Foods Not to Eat*. For foods to eat, they put a picture of a smiley face, and for foods not to eat, they put a red circle with a line through it. In the sub-branches for these topics, they put pictures of different foods. Sub-branches for foods to eat include *potato chips*, *chili*, *matzoh*, and *apple slices*. Sub-branches for foods not to eat include *sandwiches*, *pies*, *crackers*, and *hamburgers*. They put this mind map on the refrigerator so the children see it every time they are in the kitchen.

These are some of the ways you can use mind maps around the house. Using mind maps around the house helps young children understand what is going on. It presents information in a way they can understand so that they can learn routines and adapt to changes more quickly.

That wraps up Children and Mind Maps. In this section, you learned about the benefits mind maps offer children, how to teach children mind mapping, how to gear mind map lessons to the learning styles of children, and how even young children can use and learn from mind maps. Next you will learn about mind mapping software.

SECTION VI

MIND MAPPING PROGRAMS

CHAPTER 19 - MIND MAPPING SOFTWARE AND APPS

Just as word processors like Microsoft Word make it easier to write, software and apps simplify the task of drawing and creating mind maps. In fact, there are dozens of mind mapping software and apps available for computers, tablets, and even smart phones. This chapter will discuss the benefits and drawbacks of using such programs and will review some of the more popular options available.

Hand Drawn vs. Computer Mind Maps

Mind mapping using software is a very different experience from mapping by hand. Each emphasizes different thought processes, offers different options, and can be used in different ways. While the basics of mind mapping are the same, the choice of using a computer or pencil has a large effect on the final outcome. Which option is best is extremely personal, depending on both the person making the mind map and how the mind map will be used.

Process

For most adults today, drawing is intuitive. We've been drawing since we were handed our first crayon. Since mind mapping by hand is a form of drawing, it uses skills and actions we have been practicing for literally decades. We don't need to think about what we are doing—we just do it.

In contrast, using software forces us to stop and think. Very few people can control a mouse as instinctively as they can use a pen or pencil. Even those who can use a mouse will not know the controls for a new computer program intuitively until they gain experience with it. In addition, the process of controlling the program will often involve switching between different areas of the brain. Altering from manipulating a mouse (visual/kinesthetic) to typing a keyboard (verbal/kinesthetic) shifts the focus of our thoughts. This makes mind mapping on a computer more analytical than mind mapping by hand.

Options

Hand drawn mind maps are limited in terms of options. A mind map drawn by hand can include both words and shapes. You can add images, but it takes time to sketch or cut them out. You are also unable to attach electronic files like documents, audio, video, and web pages. Although mind maps can be scanned using a scanner or copied using a photo copier, they are not easy to transfer and share with people, especially people in different geographic locations.

Mind mapping programs, on the flipside, give users a lot of options. Users can pick from a wide array of branch size and color. Many programs come prepackaged with a library of images and icons users can easily incorporate. Further, most programs allow users to attach documents and other files. Mind maps on a computer can easily be saved, copied, and shared with anyone who has compatible software. These features are one of the major advantages of using mind mapping programs.

Modifying

Hand drawn mind maps are static and difficult to change. If you want to change them, your choices are limited to adding a new idea, crossing off an old one, or starting with a fresh mind map. For some people, the static nature of a hand drawn mind map is a good thing. It can keep them focused on what they have decided rather than spending hours fiddling with colors, layout, wording, etc. Others find that reworking a mind map from scratch lets them see it with a fresh perspective.

With mind mapping programs, it is much easier to edit and change the diagram long after you *finish* making it. You can move and reorder hierarchy, alter size and color of branches, vary style and size of fonts, and much more. Some software and apps store earlier versions of your maps so if you don't like the modifications, you can revert to an earlier stage and try again. Some will convert a mind map into an ordered list or embed it in a web page. Unlike a mind map made on paper, an electronic mind map doesn't ever need to be finished; you can keep coming back to it and make changes as needed.

Your decision to mind map by hand or use a program will depend on your needs in terms of process, options, and adaptability. Before making a decision, take a look at some of the available software and apps so you have a better idea of your choices.

Mind Mapping Software for Computers

Computer software for mind mapping is available for all operating systems. You can purchase and use them for Mac, PC, Linux, and other operating systems. They vary in price from free to several hundred dollars.

MindMeister

MindMeister is a free web application which has all the basic functions for mind mapping, including options for changing the colors of text and branches. It can run on any Java compatible system. MindMeister's controls allow you to build a mind map entirely from the keyboard, a great advantage for streamlined and intuitive mapping once you are familiar with the control. There are several export options including .PDF and numerous image file formats. If you upgrade to the paid version, you can also export to FreeMind and MindManager. MindMeister allows collaboration with people you designate and saves earlier versions of your mind maps for you to revert to or reference.

MindMeister has very good app versions available for both iPad and Android tablets, making it a good choice for people who need to sync mind maps across multiple platforms. It is also a great program for people looking for all the basics. While not excelling in any area, MindMeister has good functions, a variety of ways to export, and an option to collaborate.

MindManager

One of the more expensive mind mapping programs is MindManager. Its interface is similar to the tabbed setup of Microsoft Office, making it easy for Office users to learn. After installation, MindManager walks you through a sample mind map, giving you a chance to familiarize yourself with the program.

MindManager is clearly focused on corporate use. It is designed to connect and integrate with common database programs such as MySQL and Access, and it can work with MSOffice. A wide feature set allows hyperlinks, images, and attachments to be integrated into the mind map. Apps for iPhone, iPad, and Android tablet and phones allow you to make and modify mind maps on the go. This program is best for businesses or people who want to integrate a variety of media into their mind maps.

XMind

The basic XMind program is free for Windows, Mac, and Linux. There is also a paid Pro edition, but unless you need to collaborate, you'll do fine with the free version. In addition to mind mapping, XMind can be used to create logic charts, organizational trees, and other visual organizing tools. The interface is easy to use and relatively intuitive.

One nice export feature that XMind provides is the ability to embed your mind map in a website or blog. With XMind, mind maps can be exported as HTML, images, or text files. XMind apps are also available for tablets. It is the best choice for people interested in making a variety of diagrams, including maps, trees, and charts.

FreeMind

FreeMind is a Java based program and can run on any system that supports Java. As the name implies, it is available for free. Unlike many free programs, FreeMind has a large support system, including a FreeMind wiki which has information on both using the program, customizing it with keyboard shortcuts, and ways to make the application portable.

FreeMind has great visual customization with built-in keyboard shortcuts that let you build a basic mind map without taking your hands off the keyboard. Export options include HTML, PDF, and PNG. If you like to customize programs and learn every possible trick and function, you'll want to do your mind mapping with FreeMind.

Mind Mapping Apps for iPad and iPhone

There are a wide variety of mind mapping apps for Apple-based products like the iPad or iPhone. Some have an impressive list of functions and customization while others are extremely basic. Some can be easily shared and used for collaboration, but some are really just for one person. Here are four of the best mind map apps for Apple tablets and phones along with a brief description of why they may be right for you.

iThoughts

iThoughts is an app available for both iPad and iPhone. It is a versatile program that is easy to use, has good options for exporting mind maps and all the basic functions needed for making good mind maps. Over all, iThoughts is one of the best mind mapping apps available.

The ease of exporting is one of iThoughts' strongest features. iThoughts has built- in support for Box.net and Dropbox as well as desktop mind mapping applications such as FreeMind, iMindMap, MindManager, Mindview, Novamind, and XMind. The file can also be exported as a .PDF or branches of the mind map can be copied as outlines to other apps.

iThoughts also has great usability. The interface is easy to learn, making it possible to begin making mind maps almost immediately. The app has options to change the colors, icons, and shapes, so you can do everything with your map that you could if you were making it by hand. A nice bonus feature is that older versions of your mind maps are automatically saved so you can always go back to them when needed. iThoughts is a great program for people looking for an easy-to-use mind mapping app that can work with a wide range of desktop programs.

MindMeister

MindMeister originated as a web-based mind mapping tool and now has versions available for iPad, Android, and desktops. The iPad version will automatically sync up to 6 mind maps with your online account for free, but requires a paid subscription for any more.

The easy and automatic connectivity is where this app stands out from the pack, but it has other good features as well. The setup allows for easy control of colors and icons, you can link icons directly to relevant URLs, and the layout of the buttons is well thought out. MindMeister allows you to link nodes together, edging into cognitive mapping territory as well as making pure mind maps.

The functionality of the app is geared towards task-related users with features for adding due dates, priority levels, and even assigning tasks to other people with MindMeister accounts. These features combined with the automatic sync to your web account makes MindMeister an ideal option for coordinating group projects. There is one thing lacking with the MindMeister app—an *Undo* button, so you'll want to make sure you don't delete anything you will need later.

MindNode

MindNode, a bare-bones app, is mind mapping for the minimalist. The controls are automatic and easy—touch a branch and drag to create a new branch, and then type what you want it to say. There are next to no visual features—branches are all the same shape and size, though the color of the branches can be changed.

Despite its limitations, MindNode has two big advantages over other mind mapping apps. First, you can create multiple primary nodes, making it possible to create a wide variety of cognitive maps that are not possible with pure mind mapping apps. Second, and perhaps more importantly, you can print your mind map directly from MindNode, unlike most mind mapping software, which requires you to export your map to another file type and then print. MindNode is perfect for people who want quick and easy mind mapping without worrying about excessive features.

Maptini

Like MindNode, Maptini is a minimalist mind mapping app. Though this may change in the future as updates are already being prepared. Maptini has one feature no other mind mapping apps on this list have: real-time collaboration.

With Maptini, a group of people can work together to build a mind map, either by inviting contributors or making the map public so anyone can use it. The app can work collaboratively with other apps or with the desktop version. Maptini is the best app for collaborative group projects where everyone is working together to design or brainstorm.

Mind Mapping Apps for Android

Android based tablets and phones have fewer mind mapping options than their Apple counterpart. Two years ago there were practically no mind mapping apps for the Android platform. Since then, more are being developed. While Android still can't compete with Apple in number, it has enough apps with different options and features to fit your need.

MindJet

The MindJet app for Android, like MindJet for desktops, is optimized for corporate and group use. Users who don't have a desktop version of MindManager can use the MindJet Connect cloud service to transfer mind maps to any computer. Tasks in an app can also be assigned to group members and synced to other devices.

This app's features for building mind maps are basic, but easy to use with notes, icons, and colors available for customization. The mind map nodes can also link to other documents in your MindJet Connect account. If you are looking for a good mind mapping system for Android that can connect across platforms and is optimized for group and corporate use, you'll want to take a closer look at MindJet. If you want to mind map for personal use, you are better off with other options.

Mindomo

A strong all-around app, Mindomo has a little bit of everything. The interface is intuitive and easy to pick up, colors customization is built in, and it has the ability to upload images for use in your mind maps. The app comes with a free online account that automatically syncs with the app and saves a full history of your work so you can undo or redo as much as you want. The app runs when you are offline and will then automatically sync when you get online.

Two great features that you don't see in other apps are real time collaboration and layout options. Mindomo has a special menu allowing you to arrange your map in a variety of layouts with just a touch. As a bonus, you can make an unlimited number of maps and folders in which to organize them. This strong app is great for the serious mind mapper who wants mapping capability at their fingertips.

iMindMap

iMindMap originated as an iPad app, but an Android version is also available. In many ways, iMindMap comes the closest to mimicking the process of making a mind map with pen and paper. Taking advantage of the tablet touch screen, you add new nodes to a mind map by touching the node it will connect to and drawing your finger across the screen. You then name the new node, and if you want, add an icon or color.

iMindMap lacks many features that other apps have. Exporting is difficult unless you have bought the computer version; there is no way to collaborate, and unless you get a paid account, you are restricted to saving five mind maps. However the iMindMap app is the only app we've found that really uses the visual possibilities of mind maps. Anyone who is primarily a visual thinker/learner would do well to try out iMindMap for the advantages the highly visual set up provides. No other app does such a job of forming an image (rather than a chart) of your ideas.

MindMeister

MindMeister is the only program that has ended up on all three of our lists. The app for Android is similar to the web application for computers and the iPad app. It has all the basic mind map functionality—formatting options for icons, colors, and layout. The design itself is simple and easy to use. It links automatically with the web app, allowing you to save and access the mind maps from anywhere. The basic account comes with a limited number of free mind maps. As mentioned, to make and save more, you will need to get a paid account.

The one complaint some people have about MindMeister is that the app doesn't work if you are not connected to the internet, so if you will be looking to map outside of a data or Wi-Fi connection, you'll want to pick out a different app. The MindMeister app for Android is great for anyone who needs to collaborate across platforms or wants to be able to access their own mind maps from a variety of devices. It is also a good app for people who want a simple interface for making a small number of mind maps without a lot of fancy touches.

Wrapping up

From this discussion, you can see there are a quite a few mind mapping software and apps. They give you a lot of options and versatility when creating, storing, and sharing your map. The software or app you choose will depend on your specific needs or preferences. Luckily, you have many options on many platforms. So whether you are a desktop, tablet, or smart phone user, you should be able to find a program that fits your need.

SECTION VII

MIND MAP SAMPLES

CHAPTER 20 - MIND MAP SAMPLES

In the beginning of the book, we mentioned that in terms of aesthetics and design, our mind map examples are somewhat basic. If you recall, we made them this way to ensure they were easy to read. The problem with intentionally limiting our designs is that you do not get to see the versatility of mind maps. You are not able to see just how creative you can get with the technique.

In this section, we provide you with an assortment of mind map samples that illustrate the true potential of the tool. The goal of this section is to open your awareness to the endless potential of mind maps. For this reason, we provide only mind maps others have created. This way, you are not limited to seeing one person's interpretation of the technique. Instead, you are able to pull from the ingenuity and insight of other people.

Looking at the samples below will not only expand your awareness, but will also shorten the time it takes to become proficient with the technique. By simply glancing at all the varieties users have created, you will gain tremendous experience and insight. The level of comprehension you gain can take weeks to months off your learning cur. It will build up your understanding on the different applications and approaches that individuals before you have discovered. It is a great exercise that can quickly enhance your skill.

This section will be easy to go through as there are very few words, only a series of diagrams. With each diagram, pay close attention to how its designer set it up. Try to understand what he or she was trying to communicate. Look at how the hierarchies and branches are organized. If the maps have images, take notice of how they are employed.

Before moving forward, I want to point out that it is not my intention to take credit for other people's imagination and creativity. I've cited and given credit to the person or organization that created these diagrams. If there is an issue or discrepancy with the citations, please notify us so they can be corrected.

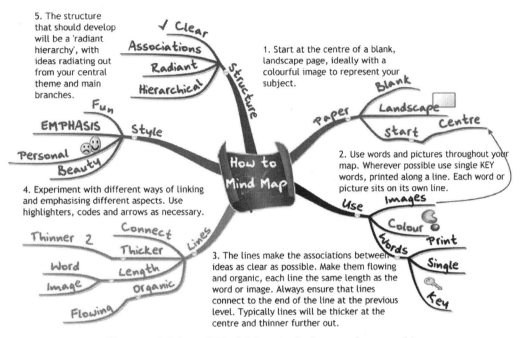

How to Make a Mind Map (mind-mapping.co.uk)

This mind map interestingly enough is about how to make a mind map. It reviews all the considerations that we have addressed. It discusses the use of images, color, and keywords. It also talks about altering the thickness of the lines as well as the different ways to organize and structure the content.

If you notice, this specific map adds a brief narrative next to each branch. In a sense, such a narrative goes against the intention of a mind map because, to a certain degree, it takes away some of its associative and visual element. However, by including the narrative, you get the best of both worlds. You have a visual representation of the content as well as a detailed explanation. This can be useful to a person who lacks extensive experience with mind maps. If a viewer is confused about a branch, connection, or hierarchy, he or she can read the narrative for added clarity.

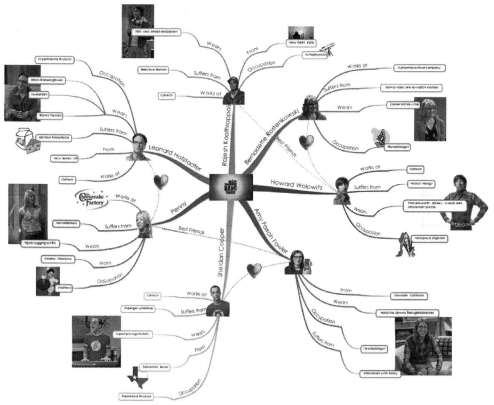

Big Bang Theory Sitcom by Nizzy

The mind map here is about the television sitcom *Big Bang Theory*. This map starts out with the logo of the sitcom in the center. From there, it lists the show's main characters as subtopics. If you notice, each subtopic includes both the name and picture of the person. From there, the lower-level topics describe details such as who the character is, where he or she comes from, and what he or she does for a living. There are even dotted lines between the characters describing their relationship to one another.

Art & Design Mind Map by Ian Gowdie

The above mind map deals with art and design. It organizes information about using imagination as a resource in developing creative thought. The Mind Map examines knowledge, experience, education, and the effects of health, culture, and social issues in art and design. I really like this one because even though it is a mind map, it actually looks like a work of art.

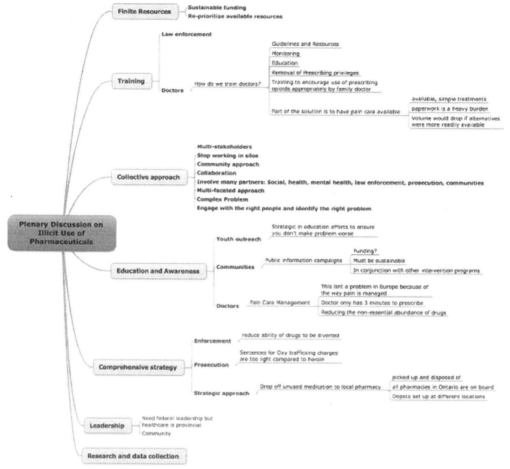

Illicit Use of Pharmaceuticals (publicsafety.gc.ca)

This mind map sample is taken from the *publicsfatey.gc.ca* website. It summarizes an article on the site about the exploitation of medication. The interesting aspect of this mind map is that the main topic *Plenary Discussion on Illicit Use of Pharmaceuticals* does not start in the center of the page, but instead to the left. As a result, all the sub and lower-level topics stem to the right. It has a very distinctive, yet professional look.

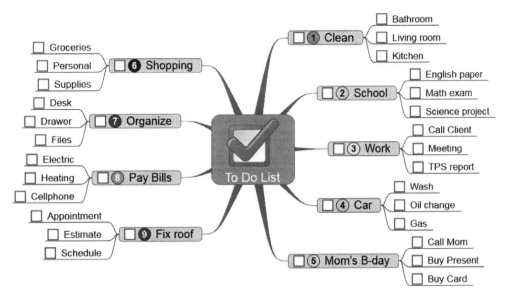

To-Do List – NovaMind Template

This is a to-do list template from a mind mapping software called NovaMind. The unique thing of this map is that there is a check-box next to each sub and lower-level topic. This is a nice feature to have because every time you finish a task, you can check it off to show that it is completed. This is a great way to put together to-do and other schedule type mind maps.

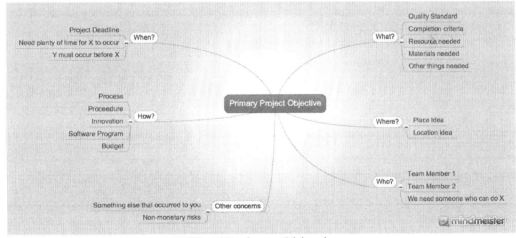

New Business Objective

This mind map sample was initially created for chapter 6 on planning. Its purpose was to show you how to use mind maps to develop a plan for a new business. However, we decided instead to use wedding planning as the example. Nonetheless, this is still a good mind map about planning, so we are including it here as an additional example of how to generate a plan with mind maps.

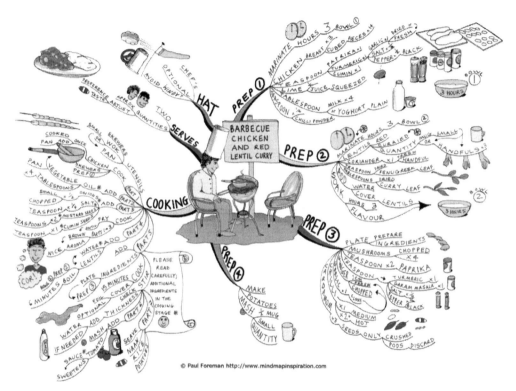

Barbecue Chicken and Red Lentil Curry Recipe by Paul Foreman
(mindmapinspiration.com)

This is a unique application of mind maps—to note a recipe. The center starts with the name of the dish, *Barbecue Chicken and Red Lentil Curry,* with a picture of a chef barbecuing. The first few branches go over the preliminary steps, which list the ingredients you will need and instructions on the initial preparations. The remaining branches provide cooking and serving instructions. Again, this is a unique way to arrange a recipe.

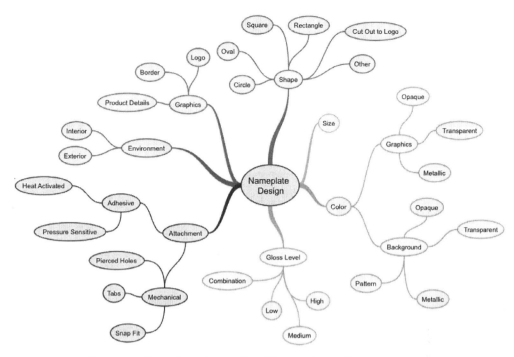

Design of Product Branding Nameplates (norcorp.com)

This map, taken from the norcorp.com website, is a checklist of things to consider when designing a nameplate. There are a couple of things to point out with its design. First, it is very basic. It uses only ovals for the main, sub, and lower-level topics. Second, this map is not content heavy. It employs very short keywords, most of them being one word in length.

Nonetheless, it does cover a lot of information. The first level branches address items you want to consider for a nameplate such as *shape*, *size*, *color*, *gloss level*, and *graphics*. Further down, you are given additional options and considerations. For example, with *gloss level*, you can choose *low*, *medium*, *high*, or a *combination*. Overall, it has a very interesting look, rather like an interconnecting web of dancing eyes.

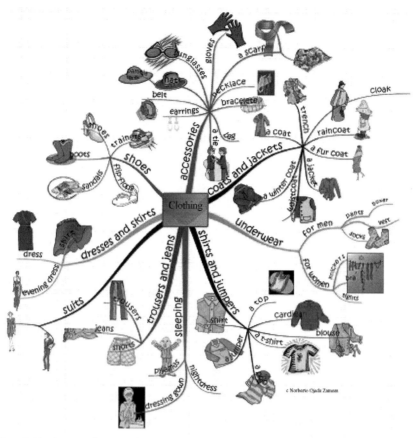

Clothing Mind Map by Norberto Ojeda Zamora (norbertoojeda.blogspot.com)

This diagram categorizes clothes. This is the type of mind map that works well with children. It takes a basic topic and breaks it down with pictures in a way that children can easily comprehend and enjoy.

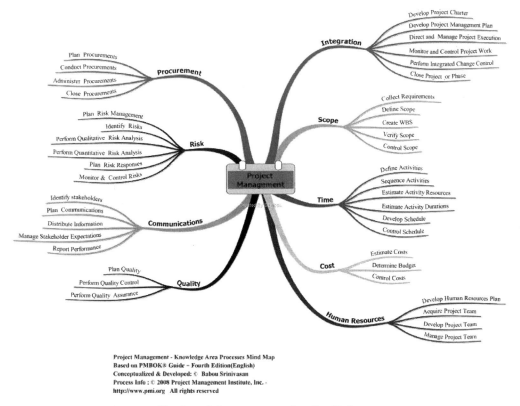

Project Management by S. Babou

This is a project management mind map developed to address an organization's requirements related to a project. The subtopics address *integration*, *scope*, *time*, *cost*, *resources*, *quality*, *communication*, *risk*, and *procurement*. These are the types of areas an organization normally needs to address when executing a project.

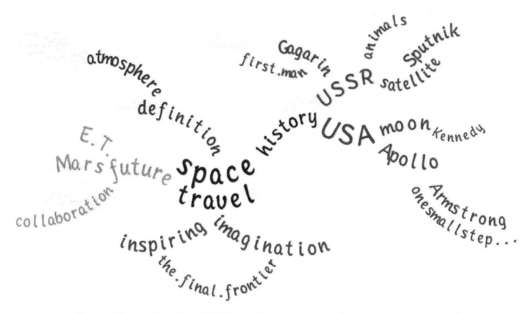

Space Travel by David Warr (languagegarden.wordpress.com)

This map is very clever in its construction. It does not use lines or shapes of any sort. Instead, keywords are written out like branches. The subject of this mind map is *Space Travel*. One of the main branches is *history*. The major players in the history of space travel were the United States (*USA*) & the Soviet Union (*USSR*), so they are appropriately noted. The lower-level branches list their respective accomplishments. USSR was the first to send a *satellite* and *man* into space. USA was the first to land a man on the *moon*.

The above examples should give you a better perspective on just how innovative you can get with mind maps. This is a tool that is truly both logical and creative.

CONCLUSION

Well, that's all I have for you as it relates to mind maps. I hope you enjoyed learning about this wonderful technique. I believe that each and every one of us has the potential to become a better reader, writer, learner, note taker, researcher, and achiever. We just need a system to show us the way. Mind map is one of the few systems that can aid us in all of these areas and more.

Though, one of the big problems I see with many mind mapping books on the market is that they do a poor job of going into detail. They will tell you that you can use mind maps in countless ways such as for planning and brainstorming, but they will not show you how. You are left to figure it out on your own. If they do show you how, they provide very plain and superficial instructions and examples. Although their instructions and examples give you a basic starting point, they do little to prepare you for real world situations.

What's more, many of these books are challenging to read and understand. They are written in a way where the information makes sense to the author or others who are familiar with the method, but is confusing to those who are new to the topic or are at a beginner level.

Thus, the goal of this book was to make the information simple and easy to learn, while providing very detailed instructions and examples. This way you can see just how robust and flexible this tool is without feeling intimidated to begin. In addition, I wanted to provide you with several variations for each use or application. Not every approach to mind maps works for everyone. Some approaches work very naturally with some people, while other approaches work better for others. Having a variety at your disposal gives you enough options to find one that works intuitively for you.

As you may have gathered, I am passionate about helping people reach their potential, whether it is in their personal, professional, or academic life. As commented earlier, I believe mind maps are one of those rare tools that can be applied very easily in all these areas. With that said, I hope you feel that this book was both simple and informative and that you found the illustrations and varied approaches worthwhile. If you did, it would be helpful if you can leave a positive review of this book on Amazon.com or the website of the retailer where you purchased the title. This will be useful in spreading the word about the technique.

I would like to conclude by reminding you to continue your mind map journey. Take what you have learned in this book and put it to use in your life. Begin right away. The sooner you start, the more experience you will gain. The more experience you gain, the better you will get at using the system. The better you get with the system, the easier it will be for you to improve memory, concentration, communication, organization, creativity, and time management with mind maps.

Suggested Reading

If you would like to explore mind maps further, the below book is an excellent guide. It set the standard for mind maps and mind mapping and discusses many innovative uses not available anywhere else including how to apply mind maps for recall and learning a foreign language.

Mind Maps: Quicker Notes, Better Memory, and Improved Learning 3.0

To learn additional ways to enhance mental performance, specifically in the area of memory, another informative book is:

Memory: Simple, Easy, and Fun Ways to Improve Memory

Made in the USA
Middletown, DE
01 December 2015